1915 Rockefeller Institute, Flexner Hall, New York, NY

1921 Peking Union Medical College, Peking, China

1921 Trinity Cathedral, Phoenix, AZ

1921 Western Reserve University Medical School, Cleveland, OH

1923 Boston Lying-In Hospital, Boston, MA

1925 All Soul's Church, Washington, DC

1925 Harvard University, McKinlock Dormitory, Cambridge, MA

1926 Harvard University, Fogg Art Museum, Cambridge, MA

1926 Vanderbilt University Medical School, Nashville, TN

1929 Rockefeller Institute, Welch Hall, New York, NY

1929 University of Virginia Medical School, Charlottesville, VA

1929 Western Reserve University, School of Nursing, Cleveland, OH

1930 Harvard University, Lowell and Dunster Houses, Cambridge, MA

1930 Memorial City Hall, Auburn, NY

1930 Rockefeller Institute, High Laboratory, New York, NY

1931 Fire & Police Station, Auburn, NY

1931 Harvard University, Adams, Kirkland, Leverett and Winthrop Houses, Cambridge, MA

1931 Lakeside Hospital, Cleveland, OH

1931 Woods Hole Oceanographic Institute, Administration Building, Woods Hole, MA

1932 Harvard University, Eliot House, Cambridge, MA

1933 Harvard University, Memorial Chapel, Cambridge, MA

1934 New York Hospital-Cornell Medical School, New York, NY

1936 Northeastern University, Campus Plan, Boston, MA

1938 Northeastern University, Richards Hall, Boston, MA

1939 Boston Blacking Chemical Company, Laboratory Building, Cambridge, MA

1939 Massachusetts General Hospital, George Robert White Memorial Building, Boston, MA

1941 Northeastern University, Laboratory Building, Boston, MA

1942 Rhode Island Hospital, Potter Building, Providence, RI

1947 Military Cemetery, Margraten, Holland

1948 Northeastern University, Ell Student Center, Boston, MA

1948 Potomac River Bridge, Washington, DC

1949 Harvard University, Lamont Library, Cambridge, MA

1951 Boca Grande Community Library, Boca Grande, FL

1952 Harvard University, Gordon McKay Applied Sciences Laboratory, Cambridge, MA

1952 Northeastern University, Dodge Library, Boston, MA

1920

1930

1940

1950

1874 HENRY HOBSON RICHARDSON 1886 SHEPLEY RUTAN AND COOLIDGE 1915 COOLIDGE AND SHATTUCK 1924 COOLIDGE SHEPLEY BULFINCH AND ABBOTT 1952 SHEPLEY BULFINCH RICHARDSON AND ABBOTT PRESENT

SHEPLEY BULFINCH RICHARDSON AND ABBOTT | PAST *to* PRESENT

JULIA HESKEL

Contents

Foreword

These few lines are in part a thank-you note from New Haven for the delightful Music Library into which Shepley Bulfinch et al have transformed a fairly dreary open courtyard in the Sterling Memorial Library at Yale. The vast new room bursts jubilantly up out of the depths of the solemn old building and is only the most striking of the several fine projects of restoration and rejuvenation which Shepley Bulfinch have carried out within it.

Their work joins that of a number of other architects who have become involved in various ambitious remodelings of other important buildings at Yale, showing how far architects have come during the past generation in being able to remodel older buildings without destroying them, how well they have in fact learned civilization's most essential lesson, how to build incrementally onto the past.

This seems especially cogent in the case of Shepley Bulfinch who, beginning as they do with Richardson, impress us as having moved seamlessly from the late nineteenth century into the present. Richardson himself was the most effective of all American architects at making the deep past live again. His buildings, like Hawthorne's stories, created a history for New England far more ancient than that history really was, and almost everything most alive in American architecture thereafter, houses and skyscrapers alike, seemed to grow out of that work — of which Shepley Bulfinch, in all their permutations, remain the direct heirs.

Their buildings after Richardson's time embody their own history of American architecture over more than a hundred years. That history had its ups and downs. Probably the most critical period came directly after World War II, when the whole continuity of European and American architecture came into question. Here the presence in the firm of Jean Paul Carlhian may have been the essential factor in charting Shepley Bulfinch's surprisingly steady course, which tended to rationalize Bauhaus fanaticism with Beaux-Arts sophistication. The Harvard Houses come especially to mind. I personally prefer Stiles and Morse at Yale to Mather and Leverett at Harvard, but it is hard not to prefer Quincy to all of them. I vividly remember how, when I was master of Morse in the early seventies and had to squeeze more students into it, I wished I had Quincy's wonderfully flexible plan of living and bedrooms to deal with rather than Saarinen's more rigid arrangement.

Moreover, if one thinks of all the architects who have worked at Yale since the eighteen sixties — Sturgis and Wight, Cady and Price, Pope, Goodhue, Rogers, Delano and Aldrich, Swartwout, Kahn, Saarinen, Rudolph, now at last Venturi — it comes to mind that they can be almost matched at Harvard over that century by Shepley Bulfinch alone. There is no solid continuity in one place quite like this one to be found anywhere else in the history of American architecture.

Vincent Scully
Sterling Professor Emeritus
History of Art
Yale University

Introduction

Tracing its roots to the arrival in Boston in 1874 of Henry Hobson Richardson, Shepley Bulfinch Richardson and Abbott is one of the oldest continuously practicing architectural firms in the United States. Richardson came to Boston to design Trinity Church in Copley Square and stayed on to build one of the most distinguished records in the history of American architecture. Today, the firm he bequeathed to his successors enjoys a national reputation for its design expertise in educational, medical, scientific research, corporate, and civic buildings.

On the occasion of its one hundred and twenty-fifth anniversary, SBRA reflects on its past to recognize what is distinctive and abiding about its journey from then to now. The salient point about SBRA's age is not that it is old, but that it remains continually vibrant and productive at the forefront of its profession. The firm's performance over time testifies to an enduring ability to grasp the spirit of the moment. This was Richardson's genius: his work caught the essence of an America in the early stages of industrialization and urbanization, an optimistic era of sudden fortunes and material expressions of worth. His buildings conveyed stability and rootedness in a world of rapid, complex change.

Today, at the dawn of a new millennium, SBRA's buildings announce stability while also enabling change in the global, networked economy. The firm's information-age libraries, for example, reflect revolutionary technological innovations as well as new patterns of socialization. In Richardson's day, a public library possessed the exclusive aura of a gentleman's club designed to preserve a particular view of culture and knowledge; today, it must serve a population diverse in origin, age, and outlook yet united in the quest to keep pace with constant change. The modern public library exists as both a place of information retrieval and a town square—a place for community participation and interaction, celebration and entertainment.

SBRA's sustained capabilities are central to Professor Scully's observation that the firm seems to have "moved seamlessly from the late nineteenth century into the present." This quality also reflects the profile of SBRA clients—and how SBRA works with them. Its clients, says the firm's president, W. Mason Smith III, are "the institutions that tie society together." These institutions are themselves products of a continuing, seamless evolution. Long noted for its work on university campuses, SBRA has created designs at Harvard, Stanford, and the University of Chicago, among many others, that embody pioneering developments in educational philosophy and mission. In keeping with the values of its clients, the firm's buildings both welcome innovation and honor tradition. This same ability to express client values manifests itself in SBRA's medical buildings, from the Rockefeller Institute to Vanderbilt Medical School to Dartmouth-Hitchcock Medical Center. In successive periods, SBRA's designs captured the state of the art in medical practice as it specialized and shifted its focus from acute illness to ambulatory care. Similarly, the firm's museums, courthouses, and public buildings capture and express America's diverse civic values at particular moments in and through time.

SBRA has been fortunate to be linked with clients seeking to learn and willing to change, and the firm has learned and changed along with them. In the firm's early days, clients and architects worked from shared cultural values. In this partnership, the client conceived a vision for his institution and the architect realized the vision for him. Today's client is typically a team composed of individuals representing diverse, and sometimes divergent, skills and perspectives of an institution. On the firm's side, the scale and complexity of most projects demand expertise not only in design but also in planning, project management and a host of related disciplines. To reconcile these multiple priorities, the firm and its clients forge close partnerships that are often formed years before design and construction begin and endure years afterward.

The organic nature of SBRA's evolution includes moments of discontinuity and change. As an institution itself, the most dramatic transitions occurred on Richardson's death in 1886, and in the 1970s, when the family firm evolved into the modern professional corporation. The death of a founder or the end of family dominance typically presents a time of trauma and peril in an organization's life. SBRA managed these transitions and thrives today because each succeeding generation respected the firm's legacy and fundamental values of design excellence, technological innovation, and commitment to meeting clients' aspirations. Yet each generation also felt—and feels—free to shape the firm's legacy and adapt its practice to changing times. The institutions that tie American society together have endured over many generations because they remain attuned to the people they serve. Understanding those institutions—where they came from and where they are going—remains vital to SBRA's enduring success.

Corn Exchange Bank Building

Virginia Library,
McCormick Theological Seminary

Art Institute of Chicago

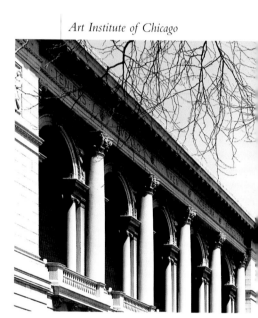

Establishing a Firm

Trinity Church

Ames Gate Lodge

Stanford University

1 | Richardson and his Successors, 1874-1914

The half-century between the Civil War and World War I witnessed profound changes for the United States and the institutions that composed its economy. Revolutions in transportation, communications, and technology transformed the country from an agrarian society to an urban, industrial nation. Mass migrations from rural areas and large waves of immigration from Europe swelled American cities, while streetcars and the automobile caused suburbs to grow up around them. A wave of inventions—the typewriter, telegraph, telephone, and electric lighting—widened business horizons. These developments in turn led to a demand for new types of construction—in the cities, civic structures, railroad stations, and commercial buildings, and in the suburbs, detached single-family houses, public libraries, and commuter railway depots.

The period that encompassed the coming of age of an industrial and urban America also witnessed the birth of the modern American architectural firm. One of the earliest of these traces its roots to 1872, when Henry Hobson Richardson won a design competition for a church in Boston. Although Richardson had submitted his entry from New York, he moved to Boston in 1874 to supervise construction. Practically overnight, the church—Trinity Church in Copley Square—established Richardson as one of the country's premier architects. Subsequently, he was called on to design many buildings for prominent institutions and individuals of the new industrial age.

During his brief 20-year career, Richardson designed buildings of practically every type imaginable: civic, religious, commercial, medical, and residential. His successors, Shepley Rutan and Coolidge, began as his apprentices. On their own, they would expand on the foundation he had built, establishing enduring relationships with the country's leading educational, medical, and civic institutions.

Trinity Church

Born on a Louisiana sugar plantation in 1838, Henry Hobson Richardson came from a distinguished line that included maternal great-grandfather Joseph Priestley, an eighteenth-century English intellectual best known for his discovery of oxygen. Like Priestley, Richardson suffered from a severe stammer. In the great-grandson's case, the impediment may have been fortuitous, if as one biographer contends, it prevented him from gaining admission to West Point. Forced to find an alternative, Richardson attended Harvard, where he joined various social clubs and developed a network of friends that included Henry Adams, Frederick Lothrop Ames, Phillips Brooks, Benjamin Crowninshield, and James A. Rumrill. This circle would provide Richardson with some of his most important building opportunities in the years to come.

On graduating from Harvard in 1859, Richardson journeyed to Paris to study architecture at the famed École des Beaux-Arts. Torn between his southern roots and northern education, he remained in France during the Civil War, after which he returned to the United States to establish his own architectural practice. Settling in New York, in 1867 he married Julia Gorham Hayden and began a family (six children over the course of the next nine years). After a brief period, Richardson formed a partnership with Charles Gambrill. With Gambrill managing the business, Richardson focused on designing churches, residences, and railroad stations in New York and New England, obtaining many of these commissions through his Harvard connections. During these years, the young architect experimented with new forms, gradually migrating from the common practice of imitating European styles to adapting those styles to American needs. The first project to display Richardson's imprimatur was also one of his finest: Trinity Church in Boston.

A New Church, a New Style, and a New Firm

Like other American cities in the early 1870s, Boston was a bustling, cosmopolitan center of business and culture. With the development of commercial activity in the downtown area, large numbers of people were moving to other parts of the city. One especially popular area of settlement was the Back Bay, a swampy tract reclaimed from the Charles River. The creation of the Back Bay presented a timely opportunity for Phillips Brooks, the new rector of Trinity Church. Having been an important fixture on Summer Street in downtown Boston for nearly a century, the church was in danger of losing its membership as people left the central city.

With Brooks leading the way, church officials decided to move Trinity Church to Back Bay and purchased a piece of land on Copley Square. In 1872, they invited six architectural firms to submit designs, including Ware and Van Brunt, Richard Morris Hunt, Peabody and Stearns, William A. Potter, and John Sturgis, who was at the time completing construction of Boston's Museum of Fine Arts. H. H. Richardson was also on the list. The architects were instructed to design an auditorium capable of seating 1,350, with "good acoustic qualities" and no columns to impede views of the preacher.[1]

Richardson's design won the competition and thus occasioned his return to the Boston environs in spring 1874. He settled in Brookline, an affluent suburb offering the right social milieu—and appropriate

Commemorative Issue, U.S. Postal Service (left)
Trinity Church (above)

"The Coops" (above)
The Staff, 1886 (left)

connections. Richardson set up shop in his house, in a studio known as the "Coops." Several young draftsmen from the New York office joined him, including Stanford White and Charles Hercules Rutan. And so an architectural firm was born.[2]

Although Richardson had a number of draftsmen assisting him, the firm was a one-man practice from its inception, with the designer having final say in all design and business decisions. One could say the same about Richardson's relationship with clients as well. A man of literally monumental personality and size (weighing 325 pounds at his peak), he was a master salesman who persuaded, cajoled, and browbeat clients to build the kind of buildings he wanted to design, often bigger and more expensive than anticipated—techniques that prompted one client to say that the architect was able to "charm a bird out of a bush."[3] Although Richardson suffered chronically from Bright's Disease (modern-day nephritis), he was by all accounts indefatigable.

In both design and execution, Trinity Church represented the result of an intense collaboration that would mark all of Richardson's major projects. During the design process, Phillips Brooks's input proved invaluable, while talented young architect Stanford White acted as Richardson's principal draftsman. During the construction phase, Richardson collaborated closely with O. W. Norcross, who soon became his master builder and established a reputation as the leading general contractor in the country. Richardson enlisted several prominent artists—among them John La Farge and Augustus Saint-Gaudens—to contribute key decorative elements.

After many iterations and revisions, the final design of Trinity Church consisted of simple geometric elements, with a low central tower dominating the entire structure, both inside and out. An eclectic blend of Syrian, Early Christian, Byzantine, and French and Spanish Romanesque, the structure exhibited elements that would become synonymous with Richardson's institutional work in the years to come. Favoring medieval design elements—asymmetry, massive walls, and rounded arches—and preindustrial materials—rough-faced ashlar stone block—the architect adapted them to suit contemporary tastes. Widely praised, Trinity Church bestowed international renown on its creator and inspired a new phase of American architecture—the "Richardson Romanesque."

Completed in 1877, Trinity became the firm's original repeat client, with several subsequent projects, including a parsonage for Brooks. Shepley Rutan and Coolidge, Richardson's successors, would design the church's West Porch and several other additions. Coolidge and Shattuck would design the baldachino as well as the pulpit, a memorial to Robert Treat Paine.

O. W. Norcross (left)
Norcross Brothers Advertisement (right)

Early Growth

In the years after Trinity's completion, Richardson undertook a broader range of projects—academic, commercial, civic, transportation, religious, and residential—in a wider range of places—Washington, D.C., New Orleans, Chicago, Cincinnati, and Wyoming. During this period, he worked on the Buffalo State Hospital for the Insane, his only medical project but one of many ventures designed in collaboration with landscape architect Frederick Law Olmsted. A large undertaking spanning most of the 1870s, the Buffalo hospital com-

mission provided a safeguard against the depression that slowed construction nationwide—and a recession-proof market that the firm would serve in subsequent economic downturns.

With the growth of suburbs in the late 1870s and early 1880s, Richardson turned his attention to building in these areas, designing detached single-family houses, small-town public libraries, and commuter railway depots. He also secured his first academic client, Harvard University, through his classmate and Brookline landlord, E. W. "Ned" Hooper, treasurer of the Harvard Corporation. Richardson's first Harvard project was Sever Hall, a large classroom building in the Yard, followed by Austin Hall at the nearby Law School. These projects marked the beginning of the firm's ongoing relationship with Harvard, which would result in hundreds of projects over the century and beyond.

Richardson also acquired a number of important individual clients, the most consequential being his Harvard friend Frederick L. Ames. Tycoons who had made their fortune in shovel manufacturing during the Civil War and the building of the transcontinental railroad, the Ames family went on to finance the Union Pacific Railroad, and in the late-nineteenth century purchased vast amounts of real estate. They provided Richardson with several important commissions, including the Oliver Ames Memorial Library and the F. L. Ames Gate Lodge, both in North Easton, Massachusetts, and the Ames Monument in Sherman, Wyoming. The relationship would continue under Shepley Rutan and Coolidge, who designed several buildings for Ames in downtown Boston.

One successful commission led to another, enabling Richardson to expand his circle of clients to prominent businessmen and other leaders outside the Northeast, among them Marshall Field and John R. Lionberger. By historical coincidence, one client, John J. Glessner, was the great grandfather of George Mathey, president of SBRA from 1978 to 1994.

To meet the growing demand for his services, in the early 1880s Richardson expanded his staff, promoting Rutan to the position of chief engineer and hiring several draftsmen. Two of the new hires soon stood apart from the rest: George Foster Shepley, a St. Louis native who had come to Boston to study at MIT, and Charles A. Coolidge, a Harvard graduate who had also gone on to MIT. As Richardson became weighed down by the growing number of projects and the increasing severity of his illness, he entrusted Shepley with responsibility for supervising the firm's projects in the Midwest.

Of all the buildings that Richardson designed in this period—many of which won high acclaim—one is universally agreed to be his best: the Allegheny County Courthouse in Pittsburgh (1888).

Trinity Church (left)
George F. Shepley (above left)
Charles A. Coolidge (above right)

Building a Civic Presence

"If they honor me for the pygmy things I have already done, what will they say when they see Pittsburgh finished?" Richardson allegedly said of his Allegheny County Courthouse—which, sadly, he did not live to see finished himself.[4] (That was left to his successors, Shepley Rutan and Coolidge.) After Andrew Carnegie built his steel mill on the Monongahela River, Pittsburgh grew rapidly, as did its need for various civic structures. In 1884, city officials commissioned Richardson to design a courthouse and jail complex.

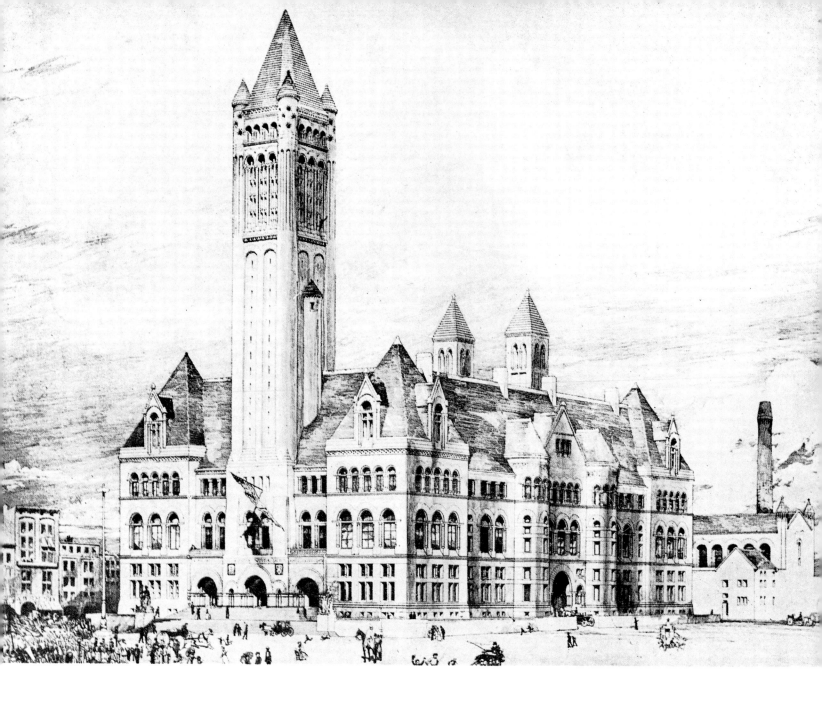

Richardson's response was both functional and aesthetically pleasing. The design, a central courtyard surrounded by a corridor leading to courtrooms, afforded ease of access, clarity of circulation, and much natural light and air. The building featured what was for the time a state-of-the-art heating and ventilation system, inspired by the Houses of Parliament in London. The main tower collected air at the top and sent it down to the basement, where it was cleaned, then warmed or cooled, and distributed throughout the building. The exterior was richly decorated by extensive use of Romanesque columns and arches. The jail followed the same design as the courthouse, but without the decorative elements; an aptly named "Bridge of Sighs" connected the two structures. Much admired in its day, the courthouse became a model for large public buildings across the country.

As the number and magnitude of commissions accelerated, so did the gravity of Richardson's illness, confining him to the Coops, and finally to his bed. Sensing the end was near, on April 27, 1886, Richardson wrote an informal will:

While I am unable to attend personally to the affairs of my office it is my wish that all my professional business shall be carried on by my assistants Messrs. Shepley, Coolidge and Rutan, in all of whom I have full confidence. In case of any question as to the control of my affairs or as to the execution of my designs the final decision must rest with Mr. George F. Shepley whom I hereby appoint as my personal representative.[5]

Richardson died later that evening. Only 47 years old, he had accomplished more in his brief career than all but a handful of architects typically accomplish in a lifetime. Delivering his eulogy at Trinity Church, Phillips Brooks spoke of the "vanishing of a great mountain from the landscape"—an apt phrase for Richardson the man, his buildings, and his impact on American architecture.[6]

Richardson left behind a multifaceted legacy: first, his buildings and a new distinctive style that adapted historical European architectural forms to newly emerging American needs, and second, his profound impact on the next generation of architects. Several trained in his studio became renowned architects in their own right: McKim and White, who with William R. Mead established one of the leading firms of the next generation; Langford Warren, who founded the school of architecture at Harvard; and Welles Bosworth, who designed MIT's campus. Architects who did not train with Richardson also felt his influence. Some imitated his style and produced Richardson Romanesque buildings in great abundance. Others, like Louis Sullivan and Frank Lloyd Wright, appreciated the broader implications of his work and continued developing a distinctly American style of architecture.

Lastly, and most consciously, Richardson left the legacy of the firm he had established—a legacy handed down to three young architects, who would complete his unfinished work and continue building the firm that Richardson had created.

Shepley Rutan and Coolidge, 1886-1915

Richardson died at the apex of his career, leaving some 25 projects in varying stages of completion, some in the construction phase, others in

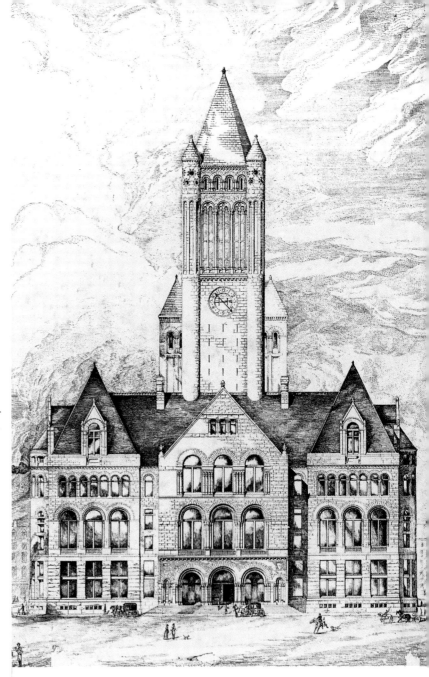

Allegheny County Courthouse (left & above)

the design phase, and still others commissioned but not yet begun. It fell to his designated heirs to complete them—not an easy burden for architects as young as Shepley (26), Coolidge (28), and Rutan (35). The three men formed a partnership satisfying certain conditions:

The firm name to be Shepley Rutan and Coolidge. All moneys received after paying the expenses of carrying on the works, including a salary of three thousand dollars a year for each member of the firm, to be turned over to [George F. Shepley] for the benefit of Mrs. Richardson, provided the amount does not exceed the sum of one hundred thousand dollars. In case the profit should exceed the above sum the excess to be equally divided among the members of the firm. All drawings now made or hereafter made to become [Shepley's] property. In case any disagreement should arise to the aforesaid work [Shepley's] decision to be final and conclusive.[7]

As the new firm name indicated, Shepley was to be senior partner. Soon afterwards, he married Richardson's daughter Julia, and the firm that was born in Richardson's home now became a thoroughly family business. Family ties were further strengthened three years later when Coolidge married Shepley's sister.[8]

Popular lore in today's SBRA has it that when Shepley and Coolidge asked Mrs. Richardson for permission to continue the work of her deceased husband, she insisted they include Rutan, whose engineering expertise was essential to the endeavor. Whatever the veracity of this story, it suggests that Richardson's heirs wanted the firm to continue providing a full range of services. Olmsted and the Norcross Brothers were to remain key collaborators.

The first order of business for the young stewards of Richardson's legacy was to complete his unfinished projects. The list included some of his greatest works: the Allegheny Courthouse and Jail, the Marshall Field Wholesale Store in Chicago, the Cincinnati Chamber of Commerce, and the J. J. Glessner House in Chicago. Each partner assumed a distinct role in the operation, with Shepley and Coolidge designing the buildings and Rutan overseeing their construction.

As these projects neared completion, the partners focused on finding new business. Richardson's connections proved helpful, but not sufficient: the partners needed to make new ones. "After Mr. Richardson died," wrote Coolidge,

I made a deal with the firm we formed (Shepley Rutan and Coolidge). I had never traveled much around the United States, and I wanted to do so, to go to every State in the Union, and to every capital city in the States; and if in this way I got any work they, of course, could pay my expenses; if not I could pay them myself. The result of this was that I got a good deal of work.[9]

Coolidge had just the right temperament for this task. "He was a man of great energy, a real promoter and organizer," noted Hugh Shepley, George Shepley's grandson and Henry R. Shepley's son. "He was very charming, and wonderful with clients."

As a result of Coolidge's travels, during the late 1880s and early 1890s the firm acquired numerous commissions—educational, commercial, civic, and residential—in San Francisco, Chicago, and Cleveland. Shepley's personal ties with the Lionbergers in St. Louis led to several projects there as well. To accommodate the workload, in the

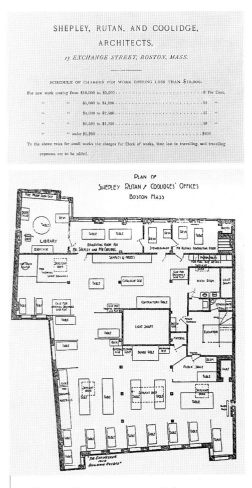

*Allegheny County Courthouse (left)
Shepley Rutan and Coolidge,
Schedule of Charges, 1890 (top)
Shepley Rutan and Coolidge,
Office at 13 Exchange Street (above)*

early 1890s the firm established branch offices in Chicago and St. Louis. (The Chicago office would remain open for 17 years, and the St. Louis office for 7.) Coolidge's entrepreneurial efforts resulted in many of SRC's most important commissions, including Stanford University (1891), the firm's first major project and first university work.

A New University, California Style

"To all who have ever frequented the arcades and courts of Stanford University, its founders' choice of architectural theme and materials seems inspired," wrote one observer many years after the university's opening.[10] Behind that inspiration lay the founders' choice of architects, Shepley Rutan and Coolidge.

Railroad titan and California senator (and former governor) Leland Stanford and his wife wished to establish an entirely new university on their enormous estate near San Francisco as a memorial to their only son, Leland Jr., who had died of typhoid fever during a grand tour of Europe with his parents. In the summer of 1886, the Stanfords retained Olmsted to develop a master plan of the proposed university, and Francis A. Walker, the president of MIT (and Coolidge's cousin) to provide advice on the needs of the different academic disciplines. They discussed the choice of architect and Walker recommended Coolidge for the job. While visiting California later that year, Coolidge met with Stanford to discuss the design of the buildings, but Stanford was not yet ready to proceed.

To formulate a new vision for his university, Stanford made a tour of American universities that included a visit to Boston. On his arrival, Coolidge introduced him to Harvard president Charles William Eliot. At the time, Eliot was consumed in revamping the undergraduate curriculum to meet the needs of the new industrial age, and was fast becoming a pivotal figure in American higher education. Coolidge recalled the first meeting of Stanford and Eliot—a "famous interview":

"Mr. Eliot, [Stanford asked] how much is your whole plant worth?" President Eliot explained to him that it was not a question of dollars and cents, it was a question much greater than that; it was a question of education, getting men together, etc. In fact he gave him a long talk about what he should do to found a university; because the Governor, at that time, had the idea to found a college where men when they graduated could immediately go out and go to work; and he did not think very much of the graduates of Harvard College, because, he said, he had them employed on a cable road in San Francisco, and they did not know enough to make change correctly! His college was to be a practical one. The result of this was that he gave me the job of making sketches for his college.[11]

In April 1887, Coolidge went to Palo Alto with his preliminary sketches and learned, much to his surprise, that Stanford wanted to lay the cornerstone on May 14, the anniversary of Leland Jr.'s birth. Coolidge later recounted the scene in some detail:

I brought some preliminary sketches to see whether the Governor would approve the plan or not. He said "Fine! – and we shall begin work next Monday." As a matter of fact I should have had a year or so to prepare for this; but I didn't say so to him, but went up to San Francisco and engaged a band

Stanford University, Inner Quadrangle (left)
Stanford University, Aerial Perspective (above)

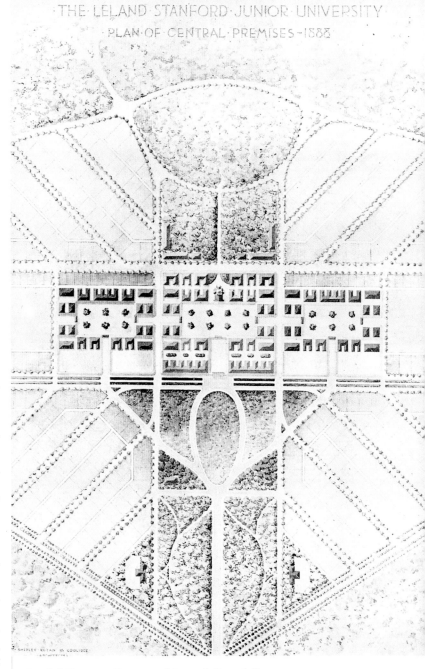

and ordered a silver spade. The Governor dug the first sods of earth, and we started in. I sat up nights to make these drawings in a little office with the engineers out there, and 2500 coolies came down to make the excavations. I made the drawings during the night, and they dug the foundations in the daytime; and that is the way the thing started.[12]

Coolidge designed a complex that suited the sun-washed, rolling coastal hills of northern California. With Olmsted's help, he created an Inner Quadrangle comprising 12 buildings that centered on a chapel and formed a huge courtyard. An Outer Quadrangle surrounded the Inner Quadrangle. The innovative design featured long arcades that connected the buildings and the quadrangles to one another, creating a cloister effect in the courtyards. To safeguard against earthquakes, Coolidge limited the height of most of the buildings to one story.[13]

When designing the exterior, Coolidge applied what he had seen in local Spanish mission churches and buildings. "I made a design for the buildings in the Mission Style, which was the first time that this was done for modern buildings," he later wrote. "Others took it up, and that was the beginning of the Mission Style in California. That was one of the things that really counted." Coolidge's choice of materials was equally deliberate: yellow Indiana limestone, which allowed for deep-cut decoration, and red tiles on the roofs.[14]

Although the design process got off to a good start, relations between Stanford and his architects became strained, owing to a dispute over who was to control the university's design.[15] In 1889, Coolidge was honeymooning in Turkey when Stanford abruptly summoned him back to Palo Alto. The architect returned, only to be kept waiting for hours and then told that Stanford was not available to meet with him.[16] Nevertheless, Coolidge supervised the execution of his design of the Inner Quadrangle, and the university opened on schedule in 1891.

After Stanford's death two years later, his widow took control of the building program, firing Coolidge and Olmsted and enlisting other architects, who designed a number of concrete buildings. Later she employed SRC to design the Memorial Arch but, despite repeated entreaties, would not allow the firm to supervise its construction. According to Rutan, Mrs. Stanford proceeded to make substantial changes in the design, raising its height and replacing the solid arch "with a thin wall reinforced with steel." The redesigned arch did not last very long, however. In 1906, a record-setting earthquake destroyed it along with several other structures on campus. The original buildings of SRC, by contrast, remained intact.[17]

The new university opened to rave reviews from academics and nonacademics alike. Stanford's buildings have a "simplicity, beauty, and fitness . . . [that] far surpassed any others which had been erected for university purposes in the United States," enthused Cornell president Andrew D. White. "When the entire plan is carried out, not even Oxford and Cambridge will have anything more beautiful."[18] While noting the influence of Richardson's Romanesque, one architectural critic praised Coolidge's "artistic power to recreate an existing type and reveal it in a finer form," while another spoke of "the Richardson style . . . handled with a boldness and imagination not typical of revivalism."[19] The design also won the praise of eminent architects, including Frank Lloyd Wright, who pronounced the quadrangles the greatest university architecture to his knowledge.[20]

Stanford University, Entrance to Memorial Court (left)
Stanford University, Campus Plan (above)

Stanford University represented an auspicious beginning for Richardson's young successors, establishing them as fully capable of following in his footsteps. It also demonstrated the firm's ability to execute substantial commissions far from home and to develop Richardson's design style in innovative and successful directions.

Boston's First Skyscraper

While the firm was doing important work on the West Coast, it was also busy with numerous projects in its hometown. Like other cities across the country, Boston was a scene of frenetic building activity. During the 1890s, Richardson's friend Frederick L. Ames hired Shepley Rutan and Coolidge to design five commercial buildings in the downtown area. One stands out above the rest—figuratively and literally. When completed in 1891, the 13-story Ames Building at One Court Street was the world's tallest office tower, as well as Boston's first elevator-dependent building. To this day, it remains the second-tallest wall-bearing structure in the country (after Burnham and Root's Monadnock Building in Chicago).[21]

Constructed by the Norcross Brothers for the then-astronomical cost of $625,000, the Ames Building is a magnificent structure reminiscent of Richardson's commercial works, such as the Marshall Field Wholesale Store in Chicago and the F. L. Ames Store in Boston.[22] It employed the latest developments in electric lighting, fireproofing, and plumbing.

On the building's completion, Shepley Rutan and Coolidge took up residence there. This would be the firm's home for nearly one hundred years—and for good reason. Listed in the National Register of Historic Places since 1974, the Ames Building remains one of the firm's celebrated designs.

While commercial projects formed a large part of SRC's Boston work, they were not the only part. During the 1890s, the railroads provided many commissions in Massachusetts, including the Springfield Passenger Station, an extension of Boston's Union Station (later renamed North Station), and a completely new terminal, South Station. The largest railroad station of its day and today Boston's main depot, South Station, Rutan's masterpiece, consolidated four different rail stations and accommodated intercity and suburban trains. Continuing another Richardson specialty, the firm also undertook a large number of residential projects in Boston and its suburbs.

Creating Civic Culture in Chicago

Home to new industries as well as to vast numbers of immigrants from Central and Eastern Europe, Chicago was another scene of the feverish 1890s building boom. Architects, both established and up-and-coming—Burnham and Root, Adler and Sullivan, and others—were at work in the downtown area, producing classical structures and cutting-edge skyscrapers, all coexisting in the cityscape.

The year 1893 witnessed the greatest building project of all, the World's Columbian Exposition, the last great world's fair of the nineteenth century, commemorating the four-hundredth anniversary of Columbus's arrival in the Americas. A celebration of America as a technological, commercial, and cultural world leader, the Exposition consisted of a series of buildings designed by renowned architects from

Ames Building (left & top)
Art Institute of Chicago (above)

North Station (above)
Corn Exchange Bank Building (left)

all over the country. Directing the building program were Burnham and the New York firm of McKim, Mead & White, the latter considered the premier practitioner of the Beaux-Arts style. Following their dictate, most of the buildings were designed in the classical mode to demonstrate the country's cultural parity with Europe. Drawing people from every corner of the world, the fair established classicism as the architectural style of the day.[23]

Two substantial commissions, the Art Institute of Chicago and the Chicago Public Library, won through design competitions, established Shepley Rutan and Coolidge as a force to be reckoned with in Chicago and in the nation. To handle these commissions, the firm established a Chicago office in 1892. According to John M. Hodgdon, whose father later became a partner with Coolidge in this office,

The local architectural talent was to no small extent upset by the loss of those prizes and to silence the uproar S. R. & C. opened the Chicago Office with the three partners taking up residence in turn for periods of a year or two. I believe the local men had good reason to wish they had remained silent about the two jobs having gone to Boston, since the presence of partners in the Chicago Office seemed to attract other work away from the old-timers in Chicago.[24]

Coolidge moved to Chicago to run operations. He would live there until 1900, and would keep a hand in its operations until 1930. In its Chicago designs, as in its other work, the firm moved away from Richardsonian Romanesque to follow the classicizing style.[25]

Built to be used by the World's Congress Auxiliary during the Exposition and as an art museum afterwards, the Art Institute of Chicago (1893) reflected the classical pattern of its neighbors—and in turn provided a model emulated by many other city art museums. The Renaissance-revival palazzo of Indiana limestone located on a prominent site on Michigan Avenue resembled "a classical building secure on its acropolis." The Art Institute was designed to house a collection of masterpieces rivaling the best museums in the country. It was "first and foremost an expression of the belief that architecture could affect social change by symbolizing and focusing the city's cultural ambitions."[26] Since its inception, the Art Institute has been a Chicago landmark.

The firm then began work on the Chicago Public Library (1897), the first civic building constructed after the devastating Great Fire of 1896. The architects once again designed a Beaux-Arts structure like those of the Columbian Exposition. The resulting library was a grand classical edifice, with round-arched windows and an Ionic colonnade. The interior was equally impressive. Renowned glass and jewelry designer Louis Comfort Tiffany created mosaics and a magnificent stained glass dome for the circulation area. SRC designed a grand staircase of Carrara marble and walls of frescoes and marble decoration throughout—affirmation of their belief that "beautiful form and colors should not be a monopoly of the rich and cultured few but the right and possession of the many."[27]

The library proved an immediate hit with Chicago residents, and with critics as well. Russell Sturgis hailed the structure as

The most important of these Chicago buildings, the most important classical composition of the time and one of the best and most spirited known to us. . . . What is so admirable in it is the free use of the some-

Chicago Public Library

what rigid classical details and classical systems of design in conformity with the requirements of the building.[28]

In 1977, the building underwent a complete restoration. The Central Library moved to a new location in 1991, and the structure assumed a new identity as the Chicago Cultural Center.

These successes—and no doubt the success of Stanford—paved the way to the firm's next major academic project. Funded by Standard Oil giant John D. Rockefeller, the University of Chicago commission—more than a dozen buildings that included Rush Medical School and the William Rainey Harper Memorial Library—kept Shepley Rutan and Coolidge busy from 1900 until World War I, and then again in the 1920s. This commission marked the beginning of two important ongoing relationships: one with Rockefeller, generating more major building complexes sponsored by the industrialist; and one with the university itself, producing subsequent projects at its library and law school. The commission also sealed the firm's reputation for academic design and led to other major university projects including the University of Oklahoma at Norman, Southern Methodist University in Dallas, and the University of Nebraska at Lincoln.[29]

During the early twentieth century, Shepley Rutan and Coolidge continued to design and build commercial buildings in an economy increasingly dominated by big corporations. With the evolution of steel frame construction and the high-speed elevator, skyscrapers took over urban skylines in cities across the country. Among its commercial buildings of this era, SRC designed the John Hancock Insurance Building in Boston and the Corn Exchange Bank Building in Chicago.

The new century had started off on a promising note indeed.

A New Age of Medicine

The late nineteenth and early twentieth centuries marked a time of great advances in medical science. European research institutes, in particular the Pasteur Institute in Paris and the Institute for Infectious Diseases in Berlin, made enormous strides that included the discovery of the tubercle bacillus.

John D. Rockefeller became convinced of the need for an institute of this kind in the United States. He donated $1 million to build a research complex in New York City and hired Shepley Rutan and Coolidge to design it. In 1906, the first building of the Rockefeller Institute for Medical Research opened its doors—with several more buildings completed over the next decade. Hailed by the *New York Herald* as the "first of its kind in America," the institute boasted facilities for primary medical research—which in those days meant "work done in laboratories, with animals."[30]

These developments in medicine coincided with continuing expansion of colleges and universities across the land. Responding to the demands of the rapidly growing and broadening industrial society, modern universities developed professional schools for medicine, law, business, and other fields like divinity and architecture. One of the leaders of this movement was Harvard's Charles William Eliot, who during the first decade of the twentieth century led the university in a major expansion of its professional schools and allied institutions. First on his list was the medical school, which

Chicago Public Library (left)
Rockefeller Institute for Medical Research (above)

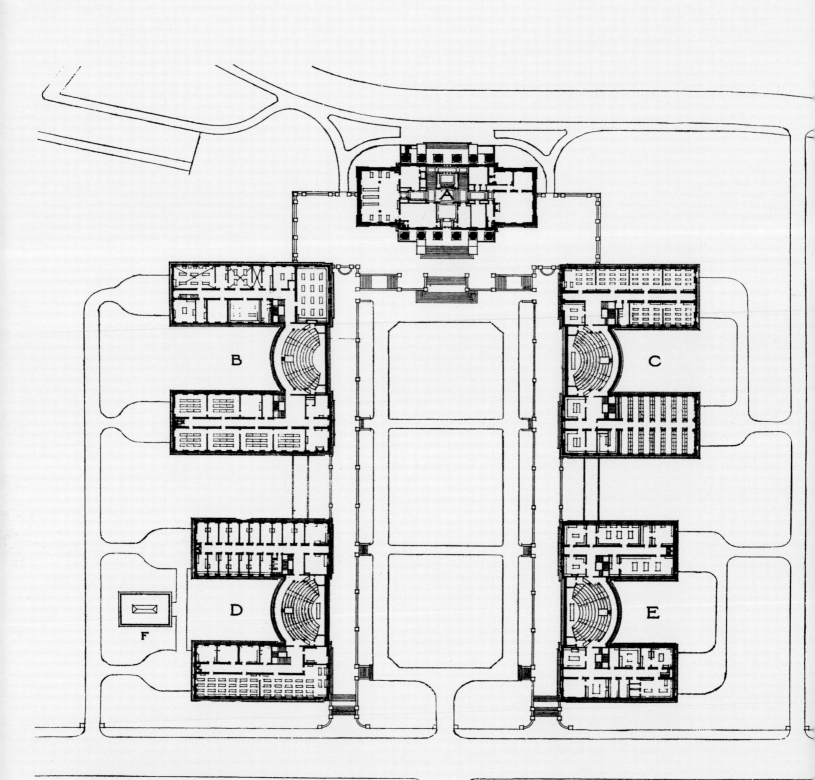

A - ADMINISTRATION BUILDING
B - ANATOMY AND HISTOLOGY BUILDING
C - PHYSIOLOGY AND PHYSIOLOGICAL
      CHEMISTRY BUILDING
D - BACTERIOLOGY AND PATHOLOGY BUILDING
E - HYGIENE AND PHARMACOLOGY BUILDING
F - ANIMAL HOUSE

PLAN OF FIRST FLOORS

needed entirely new facilities to meet the challenges of teaching doctors in a new age of medicine.[31]

Harvard University raised the bulk of its funds for the new school from four major figures in the business world. Banking magnate J. Pierpont Morgan, who had just financed the formation of United States Steel—the biggest corporation in the world in its day—gave enough to cover the cost of three of the five buildings. The widow of western rail and shipping magnate Collis P. Huntington, the Sears family, and Rockefeller also contributed generously to the project.[32]

With funding in place, Eliot hired Shepley Rutan and Coolidge to develop a design; Shepley was in charge of the design process. The assignment was deceptively straightforward: construct a medical school complex that would accommodate administrative needs as well as laboratory space for a wide range of fields: histology, anatomy, physiology, chemistry, bacteriology, pathology, hygiene, and pharmacology.

The 26-acre site in central Boston, large by any standards, meant that there would be no space constraints. Nonetheless, the assignment posed considerable challenges. First, there was a dramatic difference of 32 feet in grade at the site from the upper end to the lower end on Longwood Avenue. The solution, Coolidge later wrote, lay in placing the administration building "one story higher than the buildings which go down towards Longwood Avenue." As a result, a difference of 13 steps existed between the sidewalk and the level of the court at the foot of the terrace of the administration building, making the court appear "very much larger than it really is."[33]

Second, the buildings had to accommodate the distinct needs of the different medical areas while maintaining a uniform outward appearance. The architects met this challenge by standardizing the basement height of all the buildings and using dark colors to correspond with glass so that all the façades appeared the same.[34]

Completed in 1906, the Beaux-Arts complex consists of five imposing structures, one for administration and four for laboratories grouped in a U-shape around a long open-ended court. The four laboratory buildings have identical exteriors but markedly different interiors. According to some accounts, Yankee frugality lay behind the use of white Dorset (Vermont) marble that was originally meant for the New York Public Library and consequently was available for a very low price. Coolidge's assessment of Shepley's work still rings true:

[It] shows a direct and strong handling of the Classical style with a purity of line and simple beauty of massing that were peculiarly his own. This distinguished simplicity with little ornament but a fine feeling for scale and proportion was always characteristic of his best work.[35]

The ensemble's design provided a model for architect Welles Bosworth a few years later, when he designed the MIT campus across the Charles River.

At the same time, the new medical school complex proved an anchor for Boston's now-renowned hospital zone, the Longwood Medical area. The medical school's affiliate hospital, the Peter Bent Brigham, opened in 1913, and the Children's and Boston Lying-In

HARVARD MEDICAL SCHOOL BUILDINGS, Boston, Mass.
PANORAMIC VIEW FROM LONGWOOD AVENUE

Harvard Medical School (previous page)
Harvard Medical School, Campus Plan (left)
Harvard Medical School (above)

Hospitals, both firm designs, relocated to the vicinity soon afterwards.[36] The firm would return to the Longwood Medical area many times in the future.

No less important, the work for the Medical School represented a qualitative change in the firm's relationship with Harvard. Under Richardson, the firm had designed individual buildings in the Yard and at the Law School; under Shepley Rutan and Coolidge, it created its first complex for Harvard, and the basis of the University's medical community. In the next generation, the firm would go on to design an even larger complex for Harvard, the undergraduate residential Houses on the Charles River. (See Chapter 2.)

The Harvard Medical School complex represented Shepley's finest work—and his last. His untimely death in 1903 at the age of 43 left Coolidge with the responsibility for seeing the project to completion and for handling the rest of the firm's design commitments.

During the next decade, the firm undertook a variety of projects, mostly in Boston and its suburbs: hospitals (Massachusetts General), universities (Harvard dormitories and the Wellesley College Library), railroad depots, commercial buildings, churches, and houses. Work also continued at the Rockefeller Institute and began at a new Rockefeller-sponsored research center, the Marine Biology Laboratory at Wood's Hole, Massachusetts.

Rutan died in late 1914, leaving Coolidge as sole survivor. (He would continue leading the firm for another 21 years.) Rutan's death robbed Shepley Rutan and Coolidge of the able engineer who had supervised its construction work for 30 years.

It also marked the end of an era. The firm had seen many changes since its founding by Richardson in 1874. Made famous by a church in Boston, Richardson went on to design buildings of every conceivable kind, not only in New England but also in major cities in the South, Midwest, and even the Wild West. The impact of this prolific genius on the history of American architecture remains both indelible and incalculable.

Richardson's heirs followed in his footsteps, making modifications to suit the needs of an ever-changing American society while maintaining the firm's commitment to high-quality design and execution. Dividing responsibilities among themselves, the partners expanded the firm both numerically and geographically, acquiring major commissions coast to coast. Fundamental to this growth was the development of lasting relationships with prestigious institutions—Harvard, the University of Chicago, and the Rockefeller Institute—and eminent individuals. These included some of the most important industrialists of the Gilded Age: Frederick L. Ames, Leland Stanford, John D. Rockefeller, Andrew Carnegie, and J. P. Morgan. These relationships fostered the construction of public libraries, museums, universities, hospitals, and medical schools, and ultimately the establishment of the firm's preeminence in academic, research, and civic design.

In late 1914, the firm, like the country it served, stood on the threshold of a new era. It would be up to Coolidge, the sole survivor, to lead the firm as it adapted to the challenges and changes the new age would bring.

Shepley Rutan and Coolidge,
Annual Dinner, 1914 (left)
Menu for Annual Dinner, 1914 (above)

All Soul's Church

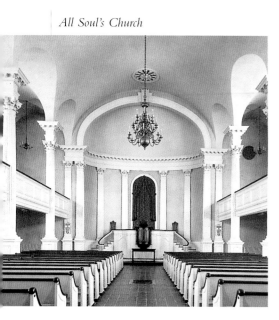

Northeastern University, Competition

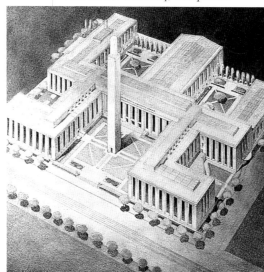

*George Robert White Memorial Building,
Massachusetts General Hospital*

From World War I to World War II

*Fogg Museum of Art,
Harvard University*

Brookline Municipal Courthouse

Insurance Exchange Building

2 | From World War I to World War II, 1914–1945

In late 1914, Charles Coolidge assessed the firm and its prospects. From all indications, the practice he had helped build over the past 30 years was in a good position to continue on the same path, making the most of the economic prosperity the United States had enjoyed since the late nineteenth century. Little did Coolidge anticipate that the firm, along with the rest of the country, was about to begin a journey through some mighty peaks and deep valleys: World War I, the Great Depression, and World War II—events that would radically transform the society the firm served.

Keeping pace with the changes and challenges these events brought, the firm—first Coolidge and Shattuck and then Coolidge Shepley Bulfinch and Abbott—focused on areas of expertise most suited to stability in turbulent times. The partners used the foundation established by their predecessors to carve out specialties in medical and academic design capable of weathering fluctuations in the economy, no matter how extreme. At the same time, they continued developing long-term relationships with great patrons and institutions and worked in collaboration with these visionaries to help them realize their hopes for American society.

Boston Blacking Chemical Company Laboratory Building

The first order of business was to fill the gap in leadership created by Rutan's death. In early 1915, Coolidge brought structural engineer George C. Shattuck into the partnership.[1] As in the past, the partners assumed responsibilities according to their talents: Coolidge was, as before, to be in charge of finding new business, while Shattuck minded the shop.

The first days of the new firm were not easy ones. Although the United States did not enter World War I until April 1917, the economy was already shifting toward mobilization. Many institutions that had planned building projects put them on hold, causing the construction boom of the past two decades to fade markedly. Coolidge and Shattuck felt the pinch at once, acquiring only a few new clients, including Trinity Cathedral in Phoenix and Yale University. The firm also managed to find work with former clients like the Maine Central Railroad Company. But far and away the most important source for new work was a new Rockefeller-funded enterprise in China, the Peking Union Medical College.

Medical Communities Abroad

Although it could scarcely be farther from Boston, the Peking Union project enjoyed origins very close to home. In 1910, Abraham Flexner had published an extensive report for the Carnegie Foundation for the Advancement of Teaching, *Medical Education in the United States and Canada*, which soon became the bible for medical education reform. Among its many recommendations, the Flexner report advocated above all that medical schools become affiliated with teaching hospitals.[2]

Influenced by these findings, the Carnegie, Rockefeller, and Harkness foundations donated millions to medical schools across the country and abroad to renovate their facilities or build entire complexes from scratch. Convinced of the need for a modern medical system in China, the Rockefeller Foundation in 1914 established the China Medical Board to oversee construction of a complex of hospital, educational, and research facilities in the city of Peking. The choice of architect was an easy one: foundation officials knew Coolidge's firm well from the University of Chicago and Harvard Medical Schools, as well as the Rockefeller Institute. That same year, Coolidge made the first of a number of month-long journeys to Peking—literally, the slow boat to China—to develop the design of the various facilities. In 1917, the complex began to take shape.

Built on the site of the former palace and garden of a Chinese prince near the southeastern corner of the Forbidden City, the Peking Union Medical College combined an up-to-date Western medical facility with an exterior that harmonized with its Eastern environs. The gray brick of the prince's palace was used to face the college buildings, while green glazed tile, reserved for the imperial palaces and temples, was used on the roofs. Completed in 1921, the complex of 14 hospital, medical school, and laboratory buildings—costing a total of $4 million, the firm's largest commission to date—constituted the partners' chief source of activity during the war.

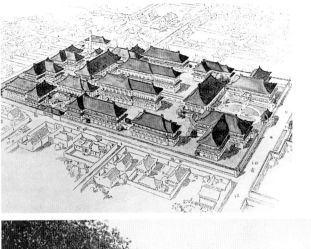

Peking Union Medical College (left)
Peking Union Medical College, perspective (top)
Boston Lying-In Hospital (above)

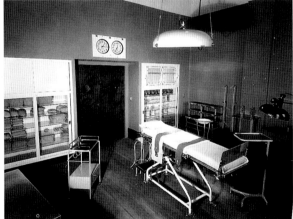

Lakeside Hospital, Western Reserve University (top)
Public Solarium (left)
Operating Room (above)

In the aftermath of the war came a deep recession that jolted the construction industry. Coolidge and Shattuck managed to keep working principally on one big project: Lakeside Hospital and the medical school at Western Reserve University in Cleveland.

The medical schools in Peking and Cleveland were a portent of things to come as soon as the economy picked up. Once an occasional area of practice, hospital design and construction would become a specialty for Coolidge and Shattuck and its successors through the years.

With the development of antiseptics and the invention of the X-ray machine and other modern technologies, in the early twentieth century hospitals were being transformed into houses of modern science—clean, efficient, and professional centers of medical treatment and nursing.[3] World War I hastened this trend, resulting in the upgrading of hospitals as centers for acute care, with the concomitant need to coordinate various specialties. No longer was the hospital an asylum for the indigent: as the practice of medicine shifted out of the patient's home, the hospital became a place where the middle class came for surgery, even of a mundane variety: obstetrical deliveries, appendectomies, and tonsillectomies and adenoidectomies. Aided by fundraising and an increasing number of bequests, hospital construction boomed, with institutions building new structures or renovating existing ones. Designed to capture the growing middle-class market, the new facilities tended to include fewer large wards and more small inpatient rooms, new diagnostic facilities, labor and delivery rooms, and other technical spaces.[4]

Alert to these developments, Coolidge made a concerted effort to enlist hospital commissions. He did not have to look very far. To accommodate the rise in obstetrical cases, the officials of the Boston Lying-In Hospital decided to relocate from the congested Massachusetts General Hospital vicinity to the Harvard Medical School area and build a larger facility that included a private ward for affluent women. Completed in 1923, the new hospital not only boasted the latest medical technology but also was the first to construct an operating room that relied on "daylight lighting."

In 1924, the Boston Lying-In won a consummate distinction: the first Harleston Parker Medal, given to the architect or firm who, in the opinion of the Boston Society of Architects, "completed the erection for any public citizen association, corporation, or public authority, the most beautiful piece of architecture, building, monument or structure within the City or Metropolitan Parks District Limits."[5]

In 1930, the firm designed Richardson House, a private wing for affluent patients.[6] The completion of the Boston Lying-In added yet another outstanding hospital to the Longwood Medical area—a process set in motion by the firm's work at the Harvard Medical School 25 years earlier—and preserved Boston's reputation as the "baby center of the world."[7] Boston had credibly reclaimed its position as medical center for the entire nation, and Coolidge and Shattuck as leading architects of medical buildings.

The Boston Lying-In was the first major project designed by Herman Voss, who was only 29 years old at the time. He was still a teenager when hired by Shepley Rutan and Coolidge as an office boy in 1908. (He would spend a staggering 63 years at the firm.) Voss's nat-

Boston Lying-In Hospital (above)
Herman Voss (left)

ural talent for sketching was immediately apparent. Jean Paul Carlhian, who was to work closely with Voss in the 1950s and 1960s, spoke of his colleague in hushed tones: "Voss was a wonderful designer with a quiet manner. He had a tremendous background based on a deep knowledge of the history of architecture. He was rational while very artistically talented." Hugh Shepley agreed: "Herman trained himself to draw with both hands. He had read that Leonardo da Vinci was ambidextrous, and decided it was a good idea: it would provide insurance, in case anything happened to his right hand."

Enter Henry Richardson Shepley

As the Lying-In Hospital took shape, Coolidge remained eager to find new medical commissions. The next major opportunity came from the South. Having obtained funding from the Carnegie Corporation and the Rockefeller Foundation's General Education Board, Vanderbilt University embarked on a program to reorganize its medical school along the lines suggested in Flexner's report, erecting a modern plant on a single campus that also included a hospital and nursing school. (The medical school at the time was located across town from the rest of the university.)[8]

The guiding force behind the project was George Canby Robinson, dean of Vanderbilt Medical School. A graduate of Johns Hopkins—the leading medical school of its day, offering the kind of medical education that the Flexner report championed—and fellow at the Rockefeller Institute, Robinson had thought long and hard about medical training. An ideal education, he believed, depended on a close interrelation between laboratory and hospital facilities that could be realized only if the different departments of the two were physically adjacent. "The physical continuity of departments," he wrote, does much "to eliminate barriers between the preclinical and clinical studies, and allows all departments to exert a constant influence on the training of future physicians."[9] Robinson's plans presented a great opportunity for the Vanderbilt medical community—and an equally great opportunity for a talented young architect, Henry Richardson Shepley.

The son of George Foster Shepley and grandson of H. H. Richardson, Henry R. Shepley had inherited an aptitude for design from both sides of the family. Like his father and grandfather before him, Shepley went from Harvard to train at the École des Beaux-Arts and then returned to the United States to practice architecture. He began his career at Shepley Rutan and Coolidge in 1914. When the United States entered World War I, Shepley was sent to France, where as a captain in the air service construction division he designed airfields at Clermont-Ferrand and Orly. After the war, he returned home and rejoined the family firm. Shepley's talent for design attracted attention, and it was not long before he was promoted to senior draftsman and key man (a combination of designer and job captain) and took charge of some of the firm's most important commissions, including Trinity Cathedral in Phoenix.[10] Realizing that the medical school–hospital complex was where the future lay, he embraced the opportunity that Vanderbilt offered.

Robinson and Shepley collaborated well together and became close personal friends. Robinson's son Otis remembered the first time he met the architect. "We were living in Nashville, near the stadium," he

Vanderbilt University Medical School (left)
CSBA Partnership notification (top)
Henry R. Shepley (above left)
Dr. George Canby Robinson (above right)

recalled. "I came home one day and found a man trimming the hedge of our house with a nail-scissors. That was my introduction to Mr. Shepley."[11] Robinson envisioned the grand plan, while Shepley's eye for detail enabled him to execute it successfully. Describing the project many years later, Robinson wrote, "He [Shepley] was the anatomist and I the physiologist, as it were, and we pooled our concepts and our understanding in a very congenial way."[12]

This collaboration produced an innovative design that realized Robinson's vision of a fully integrated medical school–teaching hospital complex. Featuring two closed and two open courts that contained laboratories and hospital wards, the structure housed everything under one roof: facilities for laboratory and clinical training of students and research facilities for their mentors.[13] Fashioned of red brick and poured concrete with carved limestone decoration, the collegiate Gothic exterior—a popular style on college campuses in the 1920s and 1930s—fit well with Vanderbilt's existing buildings.[14] Completed in 1926 (after the firm had changed its name to Coolidge Shepley Bulfinch and Abbott), the complex provided a model for other medical schools.

The Vanderbilt project cemented Shepley's reputation within the firm as a leading designer, and Coolidge and Shattuck established a reputation as experts in the design of medical school–hospital complexes. Work at the University of Virginia Medical School followed. Shepley would collaborate with Robinson on another major health care project, the New York Hospital–Cornell Medical School complex. (See below.) In the years to come, the firm would return to Vanderbilt repeatedly for work on a number of important buildings, including, in 1998, the Children's Hospital.

Coolidge Shepley Bulfinch and Abbott (1924–1952)

When Shattuck died, Coolidge was once again left as sole partner. This time, however, younger partners were waiting in the wings. According to firm lore, Henry Shepley asked Coolidge to make him a partner; Coolidge replied that if he promoted Shepley, he would have to promote other men as well. And so he did, admitting Shepley, Francis V. Bulfinch, and Lewis B. Abbott to the partnership. To mark the change, in 1924 the firm renamed itself Coolidge Shepley Bulfinch and Abbott.

This story suggests the senior partner's recognition of certain realities. To position itself in an increasingly competitive market, the firm needed partners with a wide range of expertise. Henry Shepley had already proved his great design talent in a wide range of building types—religious, academic, and especially medical. Abbott, a product of MIT like Coolidge himself, would lend design expertise in commercial work. A descendant of famous architect Charles Bulfinch and a talented structural engineer in his own right, Bulfinch was to supervise all matters related to construction.

The partners' temperaments were as varied as their skills. "My father was rather shy and not very good with clients, though he was able to transform himself if he had to," Hugh Shepley said. "He was somewhat in awe of Coolidge, who was a real charmer." Abbott, he added, was a very self-effacing, modest bachelor. Bulfinch was a different breed of personality altogether. " 'Bully' was friendly if he liked you—that is, if you were doing what you were supposed to be doing. God help you

Vanderbilt University Medical School (left)
Appleton Building, Employer's Liability Assurance Corporation (above)

if he didn't," recalled Richard M. Potter, who worked with Bulfinch for many years and later became a firm director. Hugh Shepley concurred: "I joined the firm as an office boy and ran the telephone switchboard, which was near Mr. Bulfinch's office. I'd transfer a call to him, and he'd bellow, 'Get me so and so!' He was so loud that I could hear him without the telephone."

The partners ran the firm almost as if it were four distinct operations, each in control of his subordinates and none getting in the way of his colleagues. "My father always wanted to be the sole person in charge of design," Hugh Shepley said. "He liked having a clear-cut structure, where he'd have responsibility for what he wanted to do. Bulfinch didn't get involved in design, and my father didn't get involved in engineering. They greatly admired and respected each other for their different abilities." Hugh Shepley went on to describe Abbott's role in the firm. "Abbott didn't deal with clients at all. He just sat there in his wool three-piece suit and designed. No matter how hot it got, he never took off his vest, but he never perspired. He was cool as a cucumber." Coolidge, meanwhile, continued to do what he excelled at—dealing with the firm's clients and seeking new ones. "He would call Voss in to see him and say, 'I have seven minutes before I have to meet with such-and-such client. Tell me all about the project,'" recalled Hugh Shepley. "Voss would fill him in, and he would go off and charm the client."

Although Shepley, Bulfinch, and Abbott were to work together for nearly 40 years (Coolidge would die long before his younger partners, in 1936), they stayed on very formal terms with one another. "When my father addressed Mr. Bulfinch, he called him "Bulfinch," Hugh Shepley noted. "He never called him 'Francis,' and Mr. Bulfinch never called my father 'Henry.' During my entire childhood, Mr. Bulfinch came over to the house only once, to help with some construction matter. He never came on a social basis. The relationship remained purely professional."

Coolidge's decision to promote the three young men in 1924 proved foresighted indeed. "The chief business of the American people is business," declared President Calvin Coolidge (a distant relative), and the American economy in the 1920s followed his lead. Aided by a supportive Congress, industrial production boomed, as did the stock market, soaring to unprecedented heights in the course of the decade. The newer industries—automobiles, rubber, and electricity—improved the standard of living considerably, placing washing machines, refrigerators, and cars within the reach of the average American.

In this period of growth and optimism, construction—especially commercial construction—thrived, and CSBA made the most of it. The number of office building projects rose considerably, with many projects in downtown Boston, including the Insurance Exchange Building at 40 Broad Street (designed by Coolidge and Shattuck and completed by CSBA), which in 1982 would become SBRA's headquarters. Academic construction also enjoyed a healthy resurgence, with Harvard providing several major commissions, among them the Fogg Art Museum and Langdell Hall at the Law School. But by far the largest university commissions—and the most significant for the history of education—were the residential Houses built down by the river for Harvard College.

Boston Safe Deposit and Trust Company (left)
Francis V. Bulfinch (above left)
Lewis B. Abbott (above right)

Harvard University President A. Lawrence Lowell conceived of a revolutionary idea for educating upperclassmen, which he was able to implement beginning in 1929, thanks to an $11 million gift from Standard Oil heir and philanthropist Edward S. Harkness. Specifically, Lowell envisioned the residential college. Modeled on the colleges of Oxford and Cambridge, England, the residential college, or "house," as it would be known at Harvard, was essentially a self-contained community of scholars and students, with lodgings, dining facilities, a library, athletic facilities, and common spaces.[15]

From the beginning of his tenure as president in 1909, Lowell had been concerned about the quality of undergraduate life. Whereas Charles William Eliot, Lowell's predecessor, had built up Harvard's graduate schools, Lowell focused his attention on the undergraduate college. He was determined to "construct a new solidarity" among undergraduates to replace what had been lost as student housing failed to keep pace with increased class size.[16] Lowell first implemented his vision of providing equally good accommodations for all undergraduates by building four freshman dormitories along the Charles River. Designed by Shepley Rutan and Coolidge as separate architectural entities with their own lounges, library and dining room, three of the dormitories—Gore, Standish, and Smith—opened in fall 1914. World War I then intervened, postponing the completion of the fourth, McKinlock, until 1925.

Lowell turned next to the needs of sophomores and juniors (at the time seniors were housed in the Yard). Harkness, who had long been interested in improving the learning experience of students in large schools and had served as benefactor for numerous colleges and private boarding schools, was happy to help Lowell realize his scheme. For the design and construction of the new house system in the area bordering the Charles River, Lowell commissioned CSBA.

CSBA was eminently suited for the job. The firm enjoyed a relationship with the university that dated back to H. H. Richardson's design of Sever Hall and then flourished under his successors. Coolidge, a devoted alumnus and a member of the Harvard Board of Overseers in the 1920s, enjoyed close friendships with both Eliot and Lowell. (Lowell reportedly remarked that "only Charles Coolidge was suited to design buildings for Harvard."[17]) While Coolidge played a facilitating role in the building of the Harkness Houses, Henry Shepley took charge of the design process. Like his father, whose design of the Harvard Medical School complex 25 years earlier had implemented President Eliot's vision of a pre-eminent university, Shepley would assist Lowell in realizing an equally inspired goal for Harvard's undergraduates.

The project included building three entirely new houses—Lowell, Dunster, and Eliot, all designed by Shepley—as well as bringing together existing buildings to form four additional houses—Kirkland, Winthrop, Leverett, and Adams. (This involved moving an eighteenth-century building to Kirkland House and transforming it into the library.) Each House was to be a distinct architectural complex, and all were intended to symbolize the continu-

Gore Hall, Harvard University (left)
The River Houses, Harvard University (top)
Fogg Museum of Art, Harvard University (above)

ity of Harvard's collegiate way of life by recreating the atmosphere of neo-Georgian Harvard Yard. The architects had to contend with some irregular sites—for example, Dunster House's triangle and Eliot House's hexagon.

The three new Houses were arranged around quadrangles, calling for the massing of Georgian forms in un-Georgian, even medieval, configurations. Each new House included a tower. Dunster House's tower is a classicized version of Wren's Gothic tower at Christ Church, Oxford. Eliot House's tower echoes the New York City Hall cupola of 1802, while the tower of Lowell House recalls that of Independence Hall in Philadelphia.

The architects used both the materials and the details of the eighteeth century buildings of Harvard Yard as points of departure in designing the new residential Houses. Nevertheless, they varied the color of the brick and the style of ornamentation subtly, so that each structure had its own identity. President Lowell was cost-conscious, but he also wanted the Houses to have "dignity and grace of a kind to impress and refine those who enter [their] courts, dining halls and libraries."[18] His idea was to foster intellectual life by providing congenial surroundings. Thus, the architects' interior work was as significant to the overall project as their exterior designs. For example, most of the suites had wood-burning fireplaces, and at Lowell House, the firm created nine different mantelpiece designs to help distinguish one suite from another.

Dunster and Lowell Houses opened in fall 1930. A year later, the four remodeled houses—Adams, Kirkland, Leverett, Winthrop—were ready for upperclassmen. Eliot House was completed in 1932, and Lowell's vision of the residential college became a reality at Harvard.

Critics singled out individual Houses for praise. In 1935, Lowell House garnered the Harleston Parker Medal. (According to his son Hugh, Henry Shepley himself believed that Lowell House had "the perfect proportions of a courtyard.") Noted architectural historian Bainbridge Bunting wrote that Lowell is the "largest and perhaps the handsomest of the River Houses," while Douglas Shand-Tucci described it as the "best textbook" of the residential college.[19] Dunster House also had its advocates. Critic J. D. Forbes considered it to be the most successful of the Harkness Houses, noting the "adroit handling of a difficult triangular site and a handsome composition."[20] In 1981, Dunster received the Louis Sullivan Award for Architecture, which cited, among other features, the high quality of its masonry. "[T]here is so little repetition among [the five structures facing the river] that it is surprising to discover that all were designed by one architectural firm within a seventeen-year period," Bunting noted. At the same time, he said, the design was remarkable for the visual harmony it imparted as a whole.[21]

The significance of the Harkness Houses for the firm lies in their scope and visibility. The project was one of 30 designed for the university during the CSBA years, yet it is particularly identified with the image of Harvard itself. "The Harvard houses along the river form one of Greater Boston's most majestic sights," Bunting enthused.[22] In addition to showcasing CSBA's work so prominently, the Harkness Houses deepened an enduring relationship between the firm and university.

Adams House, Harvard University (left)
Dunster House, Harvard University (top)
Lowell House, Harvard University (above)

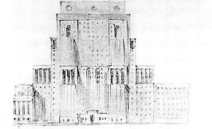
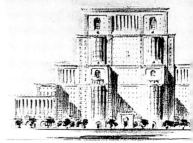

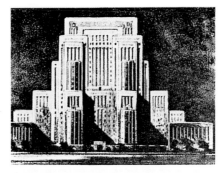
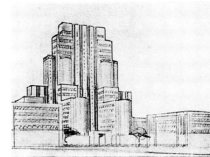
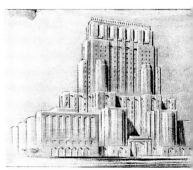
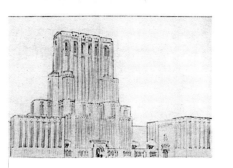

While construction in all fields benefited from the country's boom during the mid-to late 1920s, hospital construction enjoyed by far the healthiest resurgence. During this period, CSBA was inundated with projects for major medical commissions in New England and elsewhere: Boston Children's, Massachusetts General, and the University of Virginia Medical School. The jewel in the crown was the New York Hospital–Cornell Medical School complex, setting a new record for the biggest single commission in the firm's history.

Chartered by George III in 1771, New York Hospital was the oldest teaching hospital in the country. In 1928, George Canby Robinson left Vanderbilt for New York City to become director of the hospital and medical school. His first task—and one for which he was well qualified—was to head up the building of a major medical center. Turning to a known quantity, he engaged CSBA to design a hospital complex accommodating 1,000 patients and a medical school providing dormitory and recreation areas for staff, students, and service employees. To meet the demands of the project, the partners immediately expanded their staff. One of those hired in this period was designer and painter Harry Wijk, who worked closely with Herman Voss. Known around the office as "Wicky," he was remembered as somewhat emotional and temperamental. "Wijk was a sensitive designer who had a great sense of detail and color," Carlhian recalled. "His approach was more 'modern' than Voss's."

At Coolidge's behest, Voss produced some sketches of a Richardson Romanesque façade. Wanting to devise a less conventional concept, however, Shepley instructed Voss and Wijk to produce a design based on the medieval Palace of the Popes in Avignon, France. (Shepley then went off to Europe for a month-long vacation, leaving the designers to develop his elevation concepts.) Voss found some photographs of the palace. "My God, Wicky, he wants Gothic!" he exclaimed. He and Wijk enthusiastically set to work on the design. When the news of draftsmen's work reached Coolidge, he instructed Voss to return to the Romanesque concept while Wijk was to pursue the Gothic. Voss followed these instructions during office hours. Every day, however, "when 5 o'clock came, the Romanesque was put aside and the Gothic came out of hiding." When Shepley returned unexpectedly one weekend, he was greeted by an exhibition of both Gothic and Romanesque sketches. Voss's Gothic designs prevailed, and became the basis for the new medical center.[23]

An enormous complex housing five hospitals and a complete medical school, the New York Hospital–Cornell Medical School dominates Manhattan's Upper East Side—prompting one critic to remark that it is "almost a city within itself."[24] A massive pyramid dominated by a large tower, the design combines the maximum interior space with carefully planned outdoor space—a large front lawn, sunken garden, and courts of grass and trees between the buildings of the medical college ensemble on York Avenue. The exterior's only ornamentation comes from its arched windows and glazed white brick. "We were standing at the site for the hospital," Otis Robinson recalled. "Mr. Shepley lined up different samples of brick on the street. One really stood out, a glazed white brick with speckles of magnesium in it, which was very handsome. That's the one he chose." (Robinson later became the firm's brick expert.)

New York Hospital-Cornell Medical School (left)
Preliminary Elevation Studies, New York Hospital-
Cornell Medical School (above)

Fitchburg High School (left)
U.S. Parcel Post Building (below)

The New York Hospital–Cornell Medical School complex opened to unanimous acclaim. In 1932, the center won the Louis Sullivan Award for Architecture. The following year, Shepley received the Gold Medal from the Architectural League of New York for "the orderly arrangement of the many and varied parts of an unusually complex problem, and the excellence of the plan and originality of the design." Lewis Mumford hailed the ensemble as "the last smile of skyscraper romanticism."[25]

It also proved the last smile of the firm—for a long while. After the crash of the stock market in October 1929, the unbridled optimism of the past decade gave way to bank closures, breadlines, and "Brother, can you spare a dime?" Construction came to a standstill, as did CSBA's growth spurt. Its commercial practice was the hardest hit. Only a handful of new projects appeared in the early 1930s, mostly from old-time clients like Harvard, Children's Hospital, and Massachusetts General Hospital. One of the few new clients in this period was New England Deaconess Hospital. The firm's sources were drying up—and drying up fast.

The partners responded by focusing on the commissions in hand while hoping that the economy would soon recover. No one foresaw that the Depression would last for so many years. "In 1930," Hugh Shepley recalled, "Rockefeller [John D., Jr.] came to see my father. He said, 'I want you to recreate a town in Virginia called Williamsburg.' My father said, 'I'm sorry, but I'm very busy with New York Hospital and Harvard.' So Rockefeller's people went to Perry Shaw and Hepburn. That project carried them through the Depression, and my father's firm nearly collapsed."

After the New York Hospital–Cornell Medical School project concluded in 1934, little work was to be found. The firm landed only two substantial commissions, a high school in Fitchburg, Massachusetts, and the United States Parcel Post Building in Boston. CSBA went into survival mode, cutting its staff down to four and giving the newly unemployed back and vacation pay to tide them over. "My father would go to clients with his hat in his hand," recalled Hugh Shepley. "It was embarrassing to him. You didn't do that then. Architecture was an honorable profession."

In the absence of architectural work, some enterprising souls found less conventional ways to support themselves. Shepley and Voss went into business manufacturing kayaks. "My father loved boats and had wanted to be a naval architect but didn't pursue it because he thought he couldn't make a living that way," Hugh Shepley said. "Voss had actually built a boat out of papier-mâché and used it for years." The two architects modeled their design on the Eskimo kayaks hanging in Harvard's Peabody Museum—with the cockpit enlarged "to accommodate the greater girth and lesser agility of New Englanders." Sold through Abercrombie and Fitch, the boats fetched $200 apiece, a handsome price in hard times.

Shepley's time away from the office did not last for long, however. In 1935, work picked up again, and the firm rehired the architects it had let go and hired new ones. Among the new hires was James Ford Clapp, Jr., who would make a name for himself in the area of library design; two years later, the firm hired Sherman Morss, who would specialize in hospital planning.

Architectural League of New York, Gold Medal Presentation, 1932

On Coolidge's death in 1936, Shepley inherited the role of dominant partner. His watch got off to a strong start, as the number of new commissions rose rapidly. Although few were substantial, the quantity suggested that full-fledged recovery was just around the corner.

The resurgence, however, proved short-lived. In 1938, a second sharp downturn—which business leaders called "the Roosevelt Recession"—dimmed hopes of recovery nationwide, and prospects for new commissions at CSBA. During this period, Shepley struck up a friendship with Walter Gropius, the leader of the Modern or International Style, who had recently emigrated from Germany to chair the Department of Architecture at the Harvard Graduate School of Design. Shepley sponsored Gropius's application for United States citizenship and helped him find a place to live.[26] While Shepley was intrigued by Gropius's design philosophy, he also realized that it was essential to keep up with current architectural developments. "I was trained in Classical and Georgian architecture," he said. "It changed, and I had to educate myself all over again." Several commissions in the Boston area provided the opportunity. Three instances stand out as most important: the Boston Blacking Chemical Company Building, Massachusetts General Hospital's White Building, and Northeastern University.

Located on a prominent site by the Charles River in Cambridge, less than a mile from the Harvard River Houses, the BB Chemical Company Building (1939) is very much a building of its era. The firm acquired the commission because the client, Thomas Cabot, was a friend of Henry Shepley. "Cabot knew that my father was a good architect and was having trouble during the Depression," Hugh Shepley explained. "Because work was so hard to come by, my father agreed to do it."

The walls of this administration and laboratory building consist of white glazed brick, broken up with modern ribbon windows and glass blocks.[27] "Glass was the new material of those days," Hugh Shepley explained. "My father didn't trust it. He was afraid it wouldn't be waterproof, so he brought the second story out as an overhang, to protect it from direct rain." The building was a critical success. The *Boston Globe* described it as "a prime example of the modern school of Bauhaus industrial architecture."[28] Renamed the "Polaroid Building" after Polaroid purchased the building in the late 1970s, the structure was added to the National Register of Historic Places in 1982.

The George Robert White Memorial Building of the Massachusetts General Hospital (1939) serves as a crowning addition to the facilities dating back to the early nineteenth century. The fourteen-story structure of white brick complements the granite of the old Bulfinch Building, and its size and simplicity of design unify the entire hospital complex.

The most important project of the late 1930s came from an unlikely source. In 1929, Northeastern University had purchased the former training field of the Boston Red Sox on Huntington Avenue with the aim of expanding the rapidly growing institution. The Crash delayed construction for several years. Finally, university officials embarked on the process of finding architects. In 1936, they staged a competition with unusual instructions: rather than present the customary architectural rendering, the contestants were to construct an aerial view of the campus. Although the CSBA architects were at first

Boston Blacking Chemical Company, Laboratory (left)
Boston Blacking Chemical Company, Laboratory (above)

stymied, Voss soon devised an ingenious solution. He built a model, took a photograph of it, and then drew a copy of the photograph. The scheme worked. The firm won the competition—and a commission that kept it going in the last years of the Depression.

A modernist counterpart for the neo-Georgian Harvard, the Northeastern complex would consist of five sparse white-brick structures—a design befitting a technical university. The first to appear on the new quadrangle was Richards Hall, an engineering building completed in 1938, followed by the Laboratory Building three years later. The remaining three structures would not be completed until after the war.

CSBA found few other substantial commissions in the latter years of the Depression. As the firm struggled to regain momentum, world events again prompted a change of direction. With the bombing of Pearl Harbor, the United States mobilized for war, and several CSBA architects, including Wijk, Robinson, and Morss, went off to fight.

Although World War II is generally credited with spurring an American economic boom, the architectural profession did not play a significant role in this expansion. The kinds of projects that CSBA was accustomed to competing for were small in number: only a few large-scale hospital projects, including Rhode Island Hospital's Potter Building. While the firm continued to design buildings on the Harvard campus, they were mostly war-related laboratories for research in underwater sound, space acoustics, mechanical computers, and applied physics. Sparse and utilitarian, these structures were a far cry from the aesthetically compelling Houses completed only a decade earlier.

To make ends meet, CSBA engaged in a great deal of renovation and addition work, as it had during World War I—and some very small jobs, including headstones for friends and relatives of the partners. The staff hovered between 16 and 25.[29] "When the war started, work stopped again," Hugh Shepley noted. "The firm just staggered along with repair work. 'This,' my father told me, 'is why you should never be an architect.' "

In this way, the firm managed to stay afloat—an accomplishment in itself. As the last World War had shown, the question of where the firm was headed would have to wait until happier days were here again.

Northeastern University (left)
George Robert White Memorial Building,
Massachusetts General Hospital (above)

Science Center, Smith College

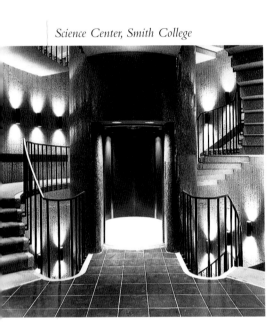

Sherman–Fairchild Physical Science Center,
Dartmouth College

Quincy House, Harvard University

Postwar Reawakening

Allston-Burr Lecture Hall,
Harvard University

Bates and Freeman Dormitories,
Wellesley College

Gordon McKay Applied Science
Laboratory, Harvard University

3 | Postwar Reawakening, 1946–1972

The end of World War II marked a major transition in the life of Coolidge Shepley Bulfinch and Abbott. Within a matter of months, years of hardship, struggle, and virtual dormancy gave way to a pronounced and prolonged revival of the architectural profession in general, and CSBA in particular. The next quarter-century would witness unprecedented growth and prosperity throughout the economy, with benefits rippling outward from major corporations, government agencies, and nonprofit institutions to the service industries that supported them.

Returning veterans came home to a world bright with opportunity. Corporations expanded to serve pent-up industrial and consumer demand in the United States and help rebuild the shattered economies of Europe and Asia. Colleges and universities swelled to accommodate vast numbers of new students, many of them supported by federal funding including the GI Bill of Rights. America's formidable capabilities in science and technology were deemed to have won the war and believed essential to maintaining lasting peace. As a consequence, massive public and private investments poured into higher education and science-based industries such as electronics and health care to ensure America's continuing global leadership. These investments, in turn, yielded stunning gains in industrial productivity and institutional performance. These were years of growing optimism, and commentators spoke confidently of the twentieth century as "the American century."

These developments would exert a profound influence on CSBA and its 1952 successor firm, Shepley Bulfinch Richardson and Abbott.

Cable Car Terminal, Squaw Valley

High Building, Hartford Hospital (left)
Perspective of High Building (below)

CSBA initially viewed the postwar economic boom with caution. Applying lessons learned during the lean years, the partners gravitated toward projects that would safeguard the practice against the next economic downturn. They took a particularly dim view of the corporate market. "After 1929," recalled Henry Shepley's son Hugh, "my father refused to do another office building. He had opportunities in the 1950s but wouldn't take them. 'Those people ran out on me in 1930,' he said. 'The people who stuck with me were the universities and hospitals, and I'll stick with them.'"

As the Peking Union, New York Hospital, and Northeastern University projects had amply demonstrated, large-scale medical and academic commissions provided stable and predictable work. These projects also enabled the firm to cultivate long-term relationships and embellish its growing reputation in these markets. After the war, these markets offered abundant opportunities.

In both medical and academic work, commissions abounded from old and new clients alike. The firm oversaw a substantial expansion of the Rockefeller Institute in New York and built a major hospital complex in Hartford, Connecticut. Work resumed at Northeastern University, where the firm added a student center, an auditorium, and several dormitories. Harvard commissioned many projects, most notably Lamont Library, the world's first open-stack facility for undergraduates.

To handle the surge of new business between 1945 and 1950, CSBA not only reabsorbed its returning veterans but also added many new hires. The size of the staff more than doubled, soaring from 33 to 79. Among the new arrivals was Joseph Priestley Richardson, grandson of the firm's founder. After studying architecture at Harvard, Joe Richardson had gone into practice on his own and established a small firm. As an officer in the U.S. Navy during the war, he participated in the amphibious assaults of Sicily, Makin Island, and Iwo Jima, and won the Bronze Star and the Meritorious Service Medal. In 1945, he joined his cousin Henry Shepley at CSBA, where he rose through the ranks and became a partner in 1950.

The partners also looked for support in less conventional venues. "Everyone was banging on my father's door, asking him to design buildings," Hugh Shepley recalled. "He had a hard time finding staff, since no one had practiced architecture for the past 15 years. So he hired some former GIs who were going to the Boston Architectural Center, trained them, and put them to work." (The firm has engaged students from the BAC on a regular basis ever since.)

CSBA also returned to an old business—transportation terminals—that suddenly teemed with new possibilities. At the turn into the twentieth century, the firm had designed many railroad stations, including Boston's South Station, the biggest terminal in the city. After the war, the rapid growth of commercial air travel prompted public officials to fund the new Logan International Airport in Boston. CSBA won the commission, which became Joe Richardson's first major project at the firm. The design maximized space for airplanes and passengers while minimizing the overall size of the complex. It featured a horseshoe-shaped structure, the Apron Building, which measured three-fifths of a mile in length and, at the time of its completion in 1953, was one of the longest buildings in

Lamont Library, Harvard University

the world. The facility boasted 16 gates and various amenities: an observation deck, restaurant, camera shop, and barber shop.

The airport made its debut to critical acclaim. "Logan Leads World in Post-War Terminal Construction," declared a *Boston Globe* headline.[1] "Now it can be said, with greater truth than ever before, that Boston has the finest airport in the world," opined the *Boston Business Journal*.[2]

Richardson's success with Logan Airport and other projects earned him not only a partnership but also a leading position in the firm. In 1952, CSBA rechristened itself as Shepley Bulfinch Richardson and Abbott (SBRA), a new identity that acknowledged both Shepley's continuing primacy and the extended family connections at the heart of the partnership. At the same time, the firm established the new rank of associate to acknowledge ability and service while fostering loyalty among young architects and giving them an incentive to move up in the firm. Among the early appointments to the new rank were Sherman Morss, an expert in hospital building, and James Ford Clapp, Jr., an expert on library design and the architect of Harvard's Lamont Library.

Formal and reserved, Morss came from an old New England family. He was highly regarded for his planning skills. "We called him 'Inches' Morss, because he could get more function into a space than anyone else," explained W. Mason Smith III, a fellow specialist in hospital planning and later SBRA's president. Morss "was thoughtful and organized, systematic and rigorous," added Hugh Shepley. "My father relied heavily on him."

Clapp, by contrast, was outgoing and enthusiastic, and by all accounts a very talented designer. "He was passionate about every aspect of design—plan, section, and elevation," Jean Paul Carlhian said. "Jimmy was a real stickler for doing things right," seconded Shepley, elaborating with a story:

I worked under him in 1958, when he was the project manager for a Harvard Law School building. The day before the bids, he asked, "Where are the window details ?" I replied, "We don't need them for bidding, and besides, we don't have the time to do them now." Clapp immediately instructed his secretary to hold all his calls, lined up a row of pencils and a sharpener, and started drawing. He stayed up all night and the next day presented us with a complete set of drawings.

As the number of commissions accelerated in the early 1950s, the firm took steps to bolster its design capabilities. Shepley appointed Voss his chief adviser on all matters of design and hired new design talent, including another new employee whose ideas would significantly alter the firm's design perspective. A Frenchman who had trained at the École des Beaux-Arts, 31-year old Jean Paul Carlhian had come to Boston to study and then taught at Harvard's Graduate School of Design. He championed creative application of modern design concepts while retaining a preference for the classical symmetry and balance characteristic of Beaux-Arts design. Although in the course of his distinguished career at SBRA Carlhian would work principally on educational projects—college residences, libraries, and student centers among them—many of the firm's other clients benefited from his influence.

In his first dozen years at the firm, Carlhian worked under Henry Shepley with designers Herman Voss and Harry Wijk. The three spent their mornings sketching in preparation for Shepley's daily reviews.

Apron Building, Logan International Airport (left page)
Sherman Morss (top left)
James Ford Clapp, Jr. (top center)
Jean Paul Carlhian (top right)
CSBA Office, 1947(above)

"We would work all morning on the eleventh floor of the Ames Building, and Shepley would come by to see what we produced every day at noon, when everyone else had gone to lunch," Carlhian recalled. "Very often all three of us would do a scheme and Shepley chose one. He trusted Herman's judgment more than Harry's. Sometimes he would let go of a project and let Voss do it." But this was more the exception than the rule: SBRA continued to be tightly managed as a small firm, with Shepley making all key decisions.

With a judicious balance of strong design talent and capable management skills, SBRA was well positioned to meet the exploding demand for architectural services in the postwar economy. Much of the new work continued to originate from longtime connections in New England. Harvard still generated the biggest academic projects, although the firm undertook significant projects for Wellesley College, Northeastern University, and the University of Massachusetts. Among many new commissions in health care, Rhode Island Hospital (RIH) proved the largest and most ambitious project of its kind and a noteworthy advance in hospital design.

Rethinking the Hospital

During World War II, remarkable advances had been made in the prevention and cure of diseases. Penicillin and other antibiotics came to enjoy widespread use, while research on gamma globulin, cortisone, and other drugs stimulated the expansion of internal medicine. After the war, these breakthroughs generated new systems of health care delivery and profoundly transformed hospital design. Gone were the long, open wards of beds typical of early-twentieth century hospitals. While the organizing principle continued to be vertical, the new hospitals of the 1940s and 1950s boasted high technology, specialized treatment units, and semiprivate rooms.[3] Rhode Island Hospital represented SBRA's response to these developments.

In 1946, Rhode Island Hospital consisted of a main structure dating back to 1867 and a collection of 15 other buildings that had sprung up haphazardly around it. Although it had long served as the acute-care general hospital for the state, the physical plant at RIH was disorganized and dilapidated, and doctors had begun to refer difficult cases to specialists in Boston. The trustees sought to address these problems, transform the hospital into a modern medical institution and make Providence a competitive hub for medical care in southern New England.

The trustees and Oliver G. Pratt, the hospital's newly appointed executive director, turned to SBRA for a solution. They were familiar with the firm, which before the war had designed the Potter Building, a pediatric facility, as well as several additions to the RIH complex. Pratt now wanted to replace the main hospital building with a structure dedicated to providing superior patient service.

Given the significance and complexity of the assignment, the firm persuaded RIH first to establish a blueprint for future building development. During the late 1940s, CSBA developed a 25-year master plan featuring a new complex with two centers, the Main Building, a new 450-bed acute-care inpatient hospital, and—in prophetic anticipation of what was to become the universal trend in outpatient care many years later—an outpatient facility that would be called the

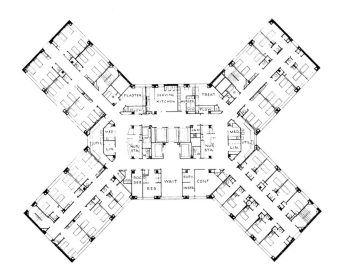

Rhode Island Hospital (left)
Patient floor plan of Main Building, Rhode Island Hospital (above)

Ambulatory Patient Center when built in the 1970s.

In 1952, work began on the Main Building. From the project's inception, the planning of this structure was an example of collaboration between two talented individuals, Pratt and Morss, each with very clear ideas about the undertaking. "The two men were very close and collaborated very well," recalled Lloyd Hughes, Pratt's successor as chief executive officer of RIH. "Morss knew hospital architecture and Pratt knew the program. Together they came up with a building that is still functioning well after 40 years."

A visionary with great aspirations for his institution, Pratt conceived of a hospital that supported better patient care while providing a more human environment. Morss believed that the new structure should be designed to emphasize flexibility and facilitate future expansion. He introduced four key planning concepts: ambitious and overstated planning targets for each department to anticipate future needs and growth; the "circulation skeleton," a network of open-ended corridors linked by strategically located banks of elevators; a zoning pattern delineating separate areas for major hospital functions—administration, inpatient nursing units, diagnostic and treatment facilities, and general services; and versatile, expandable physical space with coordinated structural and mechanical systems.[4]

The Main Building (1958) featured many innovations that created a more effective healing environment and improved operating efficiencies. The architects abandoned the traditional rectangular hospital shape in favor of a "double-Y" configuration. This plan maximized natural light and fresh air, improved patient-care efficiency on nursing units, and economized on support services. Each patient floor consisted of a centrally located elevator bank flanked by two nursing stations; two patient corridors emanated from each station. This layout reduced the distance that nurses had to walk to reach patients, enabled them to control visitor access to patient rooms, and provided a clear view of all corridors. The design also grouped patients by clinical services (medical, surgical, orthopedic) rather than by ability to pay, and featured a built-in surgical intensive care unit, one of the first of its kind in the country.

At the same time, the Main Building made an aesthetic statement. Richard M. Potter, whom Morss had hired to produce the specifications for RIH and who went on to become a firm director in 1976, described the building. "The exterior is made of white glazed brick with black magnesium specks, the same brick used at Mass. General and Northeastern," he said, adding, "It came in batches of seven, and no two bricks were alike. The mason had to lay them exactly as they came out of the box, so that the light and dark ones were scattered around."

The interior, Potter said, revealed the same attention to detail. "It has a spectacular lobby, made of very expensive Italian marble, creamy white with green veins. It is very hard to find it in a 'sincere state,' that is, without cracks that would cause it to fragment," he noted. "The interior of the chapel next door is made of white oak. Before it was finished, it was beaten with chains to make it look old and scarred. It resembles the Junior Common Room at Lowell House."

The master plan and Main Building proved only the beginning of RIH's expansion. Over the next four decades, SBRA would design a number of substantial buildings and additions, including the

Ambulatory Patient Center, Rhode Island Hospital (left)
George Building, Rhode Island Hospital (top)
Oliver Pratt and Sherman Morss (center) reviewing design progress (above)

Ambulatory Patient Center (1976), and most recently, the Hasbro Children's Hospital (1994), an entirely new pediatric facility that replaced the Potter Building. (See Chapter 5.) In the process, Rhode Island Hospital achieved its goal of becoming a preeminent regional medical center.

The Eighth House at Harvard

Higher education in the United States also benefited from the prosperity of the postwar era. The GI Bill, affordable tuition, and a growing appreciation of the value of a college degree sent students flocking to colleges and universities across the country. Using federal funds and launching their own capital campaigns, institutions of higher learning scrambled to accommodate these increased numbers and make other improvements deferred during the war. By the late 1940s, many colleges and universities had embarked on major expansion programs, increasing the size of their faculty, supporting research, and building new facilities.[5]

At Harvard, these trends manifested themselves in the imperative to build new student housing. By the mid-1950s, the River Houses were bursting at their seams and the university sought to build another house—the eighth, and the first since the completion of the Harkness Houses more than 25 years earlier. (See Chapter 2.) Once again, Harvard turned to SBRA: the firm was intimately familiar with the university's needs and recently had completed a number of Harvard buildings, including the Gordon McKay Applied Sciences Laboratory.

But SBRA's association with Harvard reached deeper than a traditional service relationship. Over the course of 75 years, the ties between the institutions had matured and grown closer. By the late 1950s, a visitor to any part of the university could not walk very far without encountering a building designed by SBRA or its predecessors.

In designing the Eighth House, SBRA faced a different set of challenges from the ones it had faced with the Harkness Houses in the 1930s. The university now had a much smaller budget: on a per-student basis, about one-third the amount spent on neighboring Lowell House in 1930. As a result, the neo-Georgian style of the Harkness Houses and the attendant amenities—separate entries, bell towers, elaborate cornices, and individual suites with fireplaces and separate studies—were simply out of the question.[6]

The initial challenge was one of location. When the idea of a new House first received serious consideration in 1955, the Harvard Corporation had wanted to build it south of Harvard Square, above the MBTA subway tracks (where the John F. Kennedy School of Government is now situated). Since only a small parcel was available for building, the House had to be more vertical than horizontal. To accommodate this requirement, Jean Paul Carlhian designed an ingenious scheme that would work in an elevator building: four-man suites arranged on three floors, with a living room and inside staircases leading to individual study-bedrooms—a design intended to increase elevator efficiency and reduce sound transmission while affording privacy and comfort.

When negotiations between the university and the MBTA broke down, planners sought a new location at the intersection of Mount Auburn and DeWolfe Streets, between Lowell and Leverett Houses.[7]

Quincy House, Commons Building, Harvard University (left)
Quincy House, Library, Harvard University (above)

Space here was also at a premium, and the project was delayed again while university officials negotiated to acquire land from local residents. Additional room was created by detaching neo-Georgian Mather Hall from Leverett House and incorporating it into the Eighth House (later named Quincy).

After close collaboration with a wide range of participants from Harvard that included masters, tutors, students, secretaries, and superintendents, SBRA designed three buildings—a dormitory block, a commons building, and a library pavilion—that together with Mather Hall would compose the new House when completed in 1959.

The three new structures demonstrated the possibilities of "form follows function" design for academic architecture. Preserving Carlhian's original plan on six floors, the dormitory block provided living quarters for resident faculty members and 360 students. The Master's suite, a penthouse complex designed by Principal in Charge Joe Richardson, occupied the top floor.

Designed by Henry Shepley, the Quincy Commons Building accommodated a wider range of activities and events than possible in the Harkness Houses. For example, although the main hall served mostly as a dining hall, it could be transformed into a theater with space for a dressing room and scenery storage. Three smaller rooms nearby doubled as private dining rooms or seminar rooms. Quincy House also boasted the first audiovisual room in a Harvard House; the space also served as a language laboratory. Facilities found in other Houses—an art studio, photographic room, and two music practice rooms—were included as well.

Between the dormitory and commons buildings stands the library, which sits on stilts, occupying a commanding position in the courtyard. The library houses a collection of 10,000 volumes and provides a place for study and leisure reading.

An International Style design rendered in neo-Georgian brick and limestone, Quincy House blended new construction seamlessly with older surroundings while making its own design statement. Carlhian organized the complex around a large courtyard like those employed by the older houses. "Shepley, who had designed Dunster House all by himself, taught me how to do the layout and size of the courtyard," he recalled. "I learned that a Georgian courtyard cannot be more than 40 feet." Carlhian also designed specific elements, such as the scale and proportions of windows, to echo those used in older structures. The folded roof on Shepley's Commons Building blended with the nearby windows of Mather Hall and Adams House. Then there were elements unique to Quincy, such as the complex fenestration, with varying sizes of windows and casements distinguishing different uses of interior space.[8]

Like the Harkness Houses, Quincy proved a critical success. In 1960, the Boston Society of Architects awarded it the prestigious Harleston Parker Medal. Critic Lewis Mumford attributed Quincy's appeal to "a careful regard for social relationships."[9]

While critics praised the complex's aesthetics, the students praised its functionality. Quincy immediately became the most oversubscribed House on campus because it offered what the older Houses did not: spacious private rooms with amenities more typical of an upscale apartment building than a college dormitory. And Carlhian became Harvard's architect of choice for dormitory design, with his Leverett House Towers and Mather House following soon afterward. In the process, SBRA reestablished its national reputation as experts in dormitory

Quincy House, Harvard University (left)
Leverett House Towers, Harvard University (above)

design. Capitalizing on the peak in demand, the firm designed a half-dozen more dormitories at New England colleges in the 1960s and early 1970s. Like Quincy House, these new buildings caught the spirit of a new era in higher education in which dormitories served not merely as residences but also as centers of community and part of the larger campus "learning environment."

A Time of Transition

SBRA's leaders understood that the 1950s represented a time of unusual opportunity and bounty—a golden era.[10] With memories of depression and war still fresh, however, they also realized that good times would not last indefinitely and that the firm would inevitably face new challenges. And meeting new challenges, they saw, would require new leadership. By late in the decade, two of the four partners—Bulfinch and Abbott—were on the verge of retirement, while Henry Shepley was increasingly debilitated with emphysema: when he made the rare visit to a client, his oxygen tank made the journey as well. (Bulfinch would retire in 1960 at age 81 and Abbott in 1964 at age 86. By 1965, all three senior partners would be dead.) To secure the firm's future, in the early to mid-1960s, the partners promoted four men from within the ranks: Clapp, Morss, Carlhian, and Hugh Shepley. (Otis Robinson's promotion followed soon afterward).

During this period of transition, Joe Richardson assumed the leadership of the firm, having learned the ropes while on the Governing Committee with his cousin Henry for several years, and, after Shepley's death, sharing the responsibility with Sherman Morss. Richardson elicited very strong reactions, both positive and negative, from his colleagues and staff: he was lovable, shy, and eccentric, indecisive yet at times autocratic. "Joe could be quite arbitrary," George Mathey, Richardson's successor, recalled. "He would say, 'That's the way it's going to be,' and that was it."

As SBRA's new leaders gained experience in running the firm in the early 1960s, academic institutions like Harvard, Middlebury, and Vanderbilt offered an array of opportunities—libraries, dormitories, and science and classroom facilities. Hospitals—old clients like Rhode Island and Hartford, and new clients like Cambridge City—kept the firm busy as well. As the number of projects continued to grow, so did the practice, reaching 120 in 1966.

During this period, each partner worked in isolation on a different floor of the Ames Building, and each was supported by a hand-selected coterie of architects. "There were all these different groups doing buildings without consulting one another," Carlhian said. The firm resembled a series of independent studios as much as a unified organization.

While this arrangement ensured each partner autonomy, it became increasingly difficult to sustain the firm's high standards of design—a problem compounded by the presence of many new, untrained staff. At Carlhian's urging, in 1967 the firm founded the Design Review Committee, consisting of two design partners and four design associates, to maintain uniformity and excellence in design.

This committee had a purely consultative role: all final decisions were left up to the principal in charge of the project. In the years that followed, the overall quality of design improved significantly—as evidenced by a new cable car terminal at Squaw Valley. A highly unusual

Mather House, Harvard University (left)
SBRA Principals and Associates, 1961 (top left)
Joseph P. Richardson (top right)
SBRA Office, 1955 (above)

project, it nonetheless illustrated SBRA's new design creativity, and to this day it remains a widely praised structure.

Expressing Movement

After Squaw Valley hosted the Winter Olympics in 1960, attendance at the northern California resort fell off precipitously. In the late 1960s, Alex Cushing, its founder and developer, was determined to restore Squaw Valley's prominence and make it a name that, like Gstaad, would be synonymous with world-class skiing. To achieve this, he planned to install the world's largest aerial tramway—designed and constructed by the Swiss firm Garaventa to carry two 120-passenger cable cars capable of transporting 1,100 skiers per hour, the largest carrying capacity of any tramway in use at the time. "The cable car system was a challenge," Cushing noted. "It was the biggest in the world. Everyone was eager to build it." But Cushing also needed a terminal to anchor the system. For that he turned to SBRA, which he knew through his friend and former Harvard roommate Joe Richardson.

Cushing's request posed a variety of design challenges for the architects. First, they had to work with a predetermined site and the specifications of a preselected tramway. Second, the terminal itself needed to move the anticipated flow of skiers efficiently and comfortably into the building, through ticket booths, and up to a boarding level high above grade to accommodate the necessary moving counterweights for the cable system. Third, it had to house and support the machinery for carrying and hauling the two cable cars some 2,000 feet in the air and over a distance of 7,000 feet. And then there were the challenges of building in California: the terminal had to be earthquake-resistant as well as fireproof.

The terminal presented an exciting opportunity for the design team to attempt something very different from its customary specialties and in a highly unusual setting. Moreover, it represented the firm's first project on the West Coast since its work at Stanford University in the late nineteenth century.

After Richardson persuaded Cushing of the merits of going modern, young architect Lloyd P. Acton conceived a bold and fresh design. Completed in late 1968, the building both displayed the machinery of the cable car system and, at the same time, provided spectacular views of the surrounding Olympic Valley in the Sierra Mountains. A glass and concrete structure, the terminal featured an entrance flanked by two transparent columns that enclosed the system's constantly moving 147-ton counterweights. Inside, skiers could move through a three-story lobby to the ticket booths and then to a 350-square-foot, glass-enclosed passenger elevator that carried 120 of them at a time to the loading level 30 feet above. From the first-level machine room to the operator's room at the top level, skiers could see the red-orange tramway machinery.

George Mathey, who served as project architect, noted, "Form follows function. The building is a piece of kinetic sculpture. Everything—except the building itself—moves," he said. Cushing agreed. "This building was not built around the machinery for the cable car system; it is an integral part of the machine. Lloyd Acton," he enthused, "made it the marvelous building that it is."

The cable car terminal instantly met with widespread acclaim. "SBRA has done an outstanding job of welding together structure, machine and mountain for the pleasure of people," *Progressive Architecture* declared.[11]

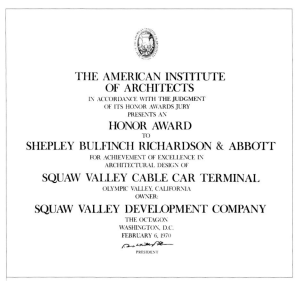

THE AMERICAN INSTITUTE
OF ARCHITECTS
IN ACCORDANCE WITH THE JUDGMENT
OF ITS HONOR AWARDS JURY
PRESENTS AN
HONOR AWARD
TO
SHEPLEY BULFINCH RICHARDSON & ABBOTT
FOR ACHIEVEMENT OF EXCELLENCE IN
ARCHITECTURAL DESIGN OF
SQUAW VALLEY CABLE CAR TERMINAL
OLYMPIC VALLEY, CALIFORNIA
OWNER:
SQUAW VALLEY DEVELOPMENT COMPANY
THE OCTAGON
WASHINGTON, D.C.
FEBRUARY 6, 1970
PRESIDENT

Cable Car Terminal, Squaw Valley (left)
American Institute of Architects, Honor Award, 1970 (above)

"Aesthetically inclined architects [like SBRA] have invaded new territory—including, of all things, Squaw Valley's cable car station," observed the *New England Architect*.[12] "The architects have imaginatively created not only a forthright terminal, they have seized on the fascination of its machinery and made of it a glass-enclosed mechanical stage set," remarked the authoritative *History of Architecture in the United States*.[13]

In 1970, the cable car terminal won a prestigious Honor Award from the American Institute of Architects and prompted the following review: "This building is ably handled, fulfilling its program well and existing, in addition, as a handsome building. It is a direct reflection of the mechanical requirements of the lift equipment and of the rather stringent demands of handling large numbers of skiers."[14] The AIA awarded Cushing a plaque as well, in recognition of his role in the erection of the terminal. "It was nice of them, but I didn't think I needed a medal for what SBRA did," he said. "An architect's design needs to meet the client's needs, and SBRA's certainly met mine."

SBRA's cable car terminal is now an icon for Squaw Valley. The electrical systems have been renovated and the cable cars replaced, but the terminal continues to house the complex. In 1998, Cushing launched development of a village, Squaw Valley USA, with the cable car terminal as the centerpiece—"much as a cathedral was in older towns," he said, adding, "The building is timeless. It has lasted 30 years, and it will continue to last."

From Family Partnership to Corporation

As SBRA entered the 1970s, the partners were well aware that the practice of architecture in the years to come would be a very different enterprise from what they had known since the war. Between 1950 and 1970, the American legal system had changed profoundly, as the development of tort law shifted responsibility from the consumer to the provider of services. From 1960 onward, the pace of litigation increased steadily, as did the likelihood of a plaintiff victory and the size of the award.[15]

In an environment in which virtually every professional service organization faced new risks, growing numbers of architectural firms sought protection through incorporation. Concerned about potential financial liability and exposure, SBRA's legal advisers urged the firm to incorporate. The partners agreed, and on October 1, 1972, the firm was reborn as Shepley Bulfinch Richardson and Abbott Incorporated. Replacing the partners were directors who practiced as principals and made up the board. An executive committee of the board, known simply as "The Committee," continued to run the business. The President, a rotating appointment, convened meetings of the board but did not take part in The Committee. To expand ownership and increase capital, each director was required to purchase stock equivalent in cost to a year's salary. Associates, in turn, were required to purchase lesser amounts of stock—the first step in a concerted move toward distributed management and collective decision making.

This legal change had little short-term effect on SBRA's internal operations, and the firm continued to operate as an "intelligently structured partnership," with Richardson in charge and The Committee handling all important business decisions. These arrangements continued until Richardson's retirement in 1978. Nonetheless, in the longer term, SBRA's new legal status prepared the way for a new generation of leaders and a different way of running the firm.

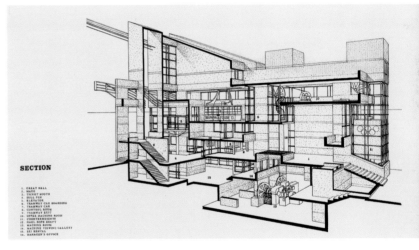

SECTION

1. GREAT HALL
2. MALL
3. TICKET BOOTH
4. BULL PEN
5. ELEVATOR
6. TRAMWAY CAR BOARDING
7. TRAMWAY CAR
8. CONTROL ROOM
9. TRAMWAY EXIT
10. UPPER MACHINE ROOM
11. COUNTERWEIGHTS
12. HAUL ROPE SHAFT
13. MACHINE ROOM
14. MACHINE VIEWING GALLERY
15. SKI RENTAL
16. MANAGER'S OFFICE

Cable Car Terminal, Squaw Valley (left)
Section through Terminal, Squaw Valley (above)

Gordon and Margaret Van Wylen Library,
Hope College

Walters Art Gallery

Andover Companies

Embarking on the Next Century of Practice

*Olin Library,
Kenyon College*

Museum of Our National Heritage

*Francis de Marneffe Library and Dining
Facility, McLean Hospital*

4 | Shepley Bulfinch Richardson and Abbott, 1973–1988

In 1973, SBRA received the prestigious Architectural Firm Award, the highest honor in the profession, from the American Institute of Architects (AIA). In the words of the Jury on Institute Honors:

The Architectural Firm Award, given only nine times in previous history, is the Institute's highest recognition for continued excellence in the work of a firm, and is awarded to an organization wherein collaboration among individuals has been the principal force in consistently producing distinguished architecture. …The firm has contributed to the best at all times during its century of practice.[1]

The accolade affirmed SBRA's remarkable achievements during its first hundred years and crowned a period of rapid growth and expanding capability in the firm. With justifiable confidence, Joe Richardson and his colleagues anticipated a bright future.

Little did these leaders realize, however, that almost at the exact moment that SBRA received the AIA award, it was about to enter a whole new age. During the 1970s, the environment for architectural services in general and for SBRA's areas of expertise in particular changed markedlly.

The performance requirements of new buildings—especially in energy efficiency—grew more exacting, and the functions of older ones were adapted to meet new uses. Clients made it their business during these years to become more active and sophisticated participants in architectural planning and design.

As building requirements increased, so did the competition for the privilege of designing them. An antitrust action brought by the Justice Department against the AIA in 1972 brought an end to fee schedules and greatly spurred competitive bidding for architectural and engineering services. Overnight, the practice of architecture, traditionally a genteel profession, faced issues previously relegated to the business world.

During the 1970s and 1980s, SBRA would adapt to these developments with the same resourcefulness and resilience it had demonstrated in the past. To meet expanding client needs, the firm placed greater emphasis on the collaborative process both inside and outside the firm, and found new ways to produce innovative, value-conscious design.

SBRA would also change the way it operated as an institution. The family-run partnership transformed itself into a modern corporation, with a diversified leadership and staff—a strategy consistent with the times it served.

Margaret Clapp Library Addition, Wellesley College

Penobscot Bay Medical Center (above & left)

In 1973, indications of a new era were already palpable. During the preceding four years, inflation, as measured by the Consumer Price Index, rose over 23 percent, causing real estate, construction, and maintenance costs to rise. The conservative tide that put Richard Nixon in the White House led to annual reductions in federal spending for social programs, including education and health care. Private contributions declined as well. The academic and medical institutions that had experienced dramatic growth during the 1950s and early 1960s now had less money to spend, and whatever money they had did not go as far.

Events of late 1973 accelerated the pace of change. The October War in the Middle East, the oil embargo by Saudi Arabia, and the quadrupling of prices by OPEC induced an energy crisis of major proportions and triggered a deep recession. By the end of the year, the Dow Jones Industrial Average dropped nearly 20 percent, while inflation reached nine percent, the highest level since World War II. Worse was to follow. In 1974, the Dow plummeted nearly 31 percent and inflation entered the double-digits. A new, unprecedented combination of low growth and high inflation—or "stagflation," as it was referred to in those days—sealed the conclusion of the 25-year postwar economic boom.

While prospects were bad for architects nationwide, the mix of runaway inflation, reduced federal funding, and shrinking university endowments proved especially challenging to SBRA. "Today times not only look bad, they are bad," read one Richardson memo.[2] So began a period that, by all accounts, was the worst SBRA had seen since the Depression. Rising to the challenge, the firm would undertake fundamental changes in every facet of its operation—design, project management, client relations, and firm governance. It would, in short, transform the way it practiced architecture. This new approach was evident in two projects of the early 1970s.

Portents of Change: the Hospital

In the early 1970s, the medical establishment of Rockland, Maine approached SBRA with a not out-of-the-ordinary request: "a good, functional medical facility design that ... [was] both economical and pleasing to the eye." Thanks to the convergence of two factors—a coastal setting free of the space constraints faced by urban hospitals, and a change in SBRA leadership during the design process—the response was anything but ordinary. The Penobscot Bay Medical Center (1975), SBRA's first from-the-ground-up hospital project in nearly 20 years, was a milestone in health care design for the firm and the model for a number of important hospital projects, including the Dartmouth-Hitchcock Medical Center and the Hasbro Children's Hospital. (See Chapter 5.)

The initial design, developed under senior architect Sherman Morss, followed the pattern of his previous hospitals, which were high-rise structures with a vertical zoning pattern. As the design was taking shape, however, Morss took a much-deserved sabbatical. James Clapp assumed temporary leadership of the project and design responsibility passed to two young architects: Lloyd Acton, winner of the recent AIA award for Squaw Valley, and Mason Smith, a specialist in hospital planning.

American Institute of Architects, Architectural Firm Award, 1973 (below) Joseph Richardson, Jean Paul Carlhian and Hugh Shepley receiving the firm award from the AIA (bottom)

THE AMERICAN INSTITUTE OF ARCHITECTS
IS HONORED TO CONFER THE
1973 ARCHITECTURAL FIRM AWARD
ON
SHEPLEY BULFINCH RICHARDSON AND ABBOTT

A FIRM WHICH HAS NOT
ONLY PRODUCED CONSISTENTLY
DISTINGUISHED ARCHITECTURE
SINCE ITS BEGINNINGS ALMOST
A CENTURY AGO, BUT WHICH
HAS ALSO SERVED AS A TRAINING
GROUND FOR YOUNG PRACTITIONERS
IN THE FINEST TRADITION OF THE
ARCHITECTURAL PROFESSION.

MAY 1973

f. Scott Ferber Jr.
PRESIDENT

Hilliard J. Smith Jr.
SECRETARY

Acton and Smith made the most of their opportunity. Taking advantage of the spacious site, they replaced Morss's vertical zoning plan with a horizontal one. This innovation enabled each area of the hospital to expand independently, thus offering greater flexibility than was possible in vertical plans. "We left a generous amount of space between service and treatment areas, so they could expand toward each other," Smith recalled. "The result was a more versatile design." This arrangement also made it possible to use the most appropriate structural system for each part of the hospital: moderate-length, 33-foot square bays for treatment and support areas, and shorter, 22-foot spans for nursing areas. Combined with a flexible, clear system of extendable corridors, the new configuration enabled the 100-bed hospital to triple its capacity.

Although SBRA did not face spatial constraints, the financial constraints were palpable. "Since it was a one-story building, we could meet the fire codes with lightweight construction," Smith explained. "Jim Clapp called it 'shopping center construction,' because it was inexpensive."

Pen Bay demonstrated SBRA's continued ability to meet the client's design requirements while observing a tight budget. No less important, the project represented a distinct move by the firm toward a more modern aesthetic, and to health care facility planning that emphasized community and a patient-focused healing environment. The building's panelized stucco exterior is at ease in its coastal setting. Its interior is filled with natural light, thanks to two-story high corridors with clerestory windows. The structure is a "rare demonstration of exuberance without excess," wrote *Architectural Record*. "…Its validity as a work of architecture, and as a hospital 'job,' has as much to do with the plain-spoken Maine-like veracity of its configuration as with the skilled arrangement of complex functions inside. …[It is] a perceptive architectural expression of wellness."[3]

In the years that followed, the features that made Pen Bay distinctive—its straightforward design approach, patient-oriented interiors, high degree of flexibility, and low cost—would continue to constitute essential elements of SBRA health care design, and its designers, Acton and Smith, would go on to positions of leadership in the firm.

Renewing the Campus

During the early 1970s, SBRA also adapted to changes occurring in its other core market, the world of higher education. While federal cutbacks had all but eliminated a major source of revenues, an impending demographic shift would soon make things worse—the decline in the number of 18-year olds in the population as the last of the baby boomers graduated from college. With costs outpacing income, the financial position of universities, particularly private ones, rapidly deteriorated. As "recycling" became a significant cultural value, a growing number of academic institutions decided to renovate or add to existing buildings rather than build new ones. In this era of belt-tightening, SBRA took on a rising volume of assignments that featured additions or renovations. The College Center of Vassar College in Poughkeepsie, New York (1976) is one such example.

Soon after Vassar College's founding in 1861, John Renwick, Jr.,

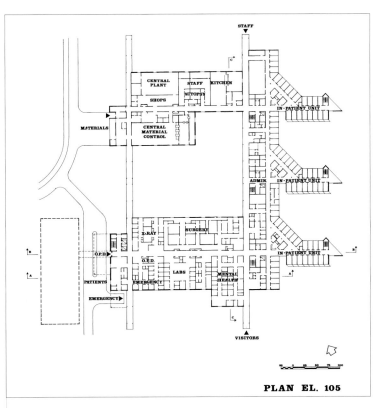

PLAN EL. 105

Penobscot Bay Medical Center (left)
Penobscot Bay Medical Center, floor plan (above)

architect of the Smithsonian Institute and St. Patrick's Cathedral in New York, designed the Main Hall. This French Second Empire structure housed all of the college's activities, including a dormitory, dining facilities, and the chapel. One hundred-odd years later, Vassar needed a building that would accommodate the changes in student life that had occurred since then: a campus center for student activities, lounges, a snack bar, post office, and an exhibition gallery. "The issue," design principal Jean Paul Carlhian explained, "was to build an addition to what in the 1860s was one of the largest buildings in New York, a building that housed everything in the college. This was the heart of the college and its most precious building."

SBRA posited one fundamental objective, to preserve the spirit of the existing architecture. Employing Renwick's compositional strategy—a balanced, symmetrical design—they devised a U-shaped modern structure wrapped around the east wing of the old building, a design that acknowledged and reinforced the original concept. To mark the transition between old and new, they designed two great glass-roofed atria, flooding the space with light and creating a sense of community—the new heart of the Vassar campus.[4]

The clearly contemporary addition displayed a keen awareness of the historic original. Since it would have been difficult to reproduce the fenestration of the Renwick building, SBRA used skylights throughout and limited all openings to large glass panes between the brick panels—a solution that provided more space uninterrupted by windows without losing natural light. The twentieth-century brick matched the nineteenth-century brick in color and coursing, and the exposed metal roof was painted gray to recall the shading of the original slate roof.[5] The new building thus peacefully coexisted with its historic core.

The College Center opened to rave reviews. The new center provides "a new moral uplift" for the community," wrote the *Poughkeepsie Observer*.[6] In 1977, the College Center received an AIA Honor Award for design excellence. According to the jury, "a carefully designed building of uncompromising modern design wrapped around this fine mid-19th century building succeeds in respecting the old building and bringing new life to the restored structure."[7]

During the early and mid-1970s, SBRA designed numerous building additions and renovations.[8] Like Vassar, the clients tended to be academic institutions, such as Wellesley with its Margaret Clapp Library East Wing, the firm's second major addition to the original Shepley Rutan and Coolidge building of 1909. Occasionally, some nonacademic clients—also feeling the financial pinch of the times—preferred an addition to a new building, as was the case with the Walters Art Gallery in Baltimore and the Andover Savings Bank in Andover, Massachusetts.

Accommodating a New Environment

When the bottom dropped out in late 1973, SBRA, like organizations everywhere, shifted into survival mode. The firm immediately scaled back salaries and hours, which dropped to a 30-hour four-day week—an arrangement that provided an entire day for moonlighting. SBRA also endured a major downscaling: by the end of 1975, the staff was reduced to 49, the lowest since 1946. Years later Richardson would write that the "the recession of 1974 was a terrible blow to all archi-

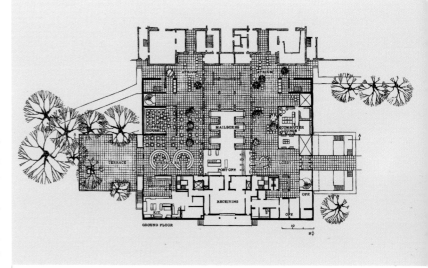

College Center, Vassar College (left)
Floor plan of the College Center (above)

tects. We sacrificed to survive and at the same time built up our reserves while earning recognition in design."[9]

To meet the challenges of these years, SBRA carried out significant management changes embodied in the principles of the 1972 incorporation. The first step was to place the firm in the hands of the new generation. In late 1973, Joe Richardson created the position of Associate Vice President—a corporate title reflecting the firm's recent metamorphosis—and promoted six of the firm's most promising associates: George Mathey, Lloyd Acton, Mason Smith, Gerrit Zwart, Daniel Coolidge (the grandson of Charles A.), and Paul Sun. When Richardson and his colleagues—Clapp and Morss, also in their sixties—retired, their successors would be ready and able to take over.

Led by Mathey, the AVPs, as they were called, spearheaded several reforms. Project teams were to have three leaders, representing the areas of management, design, and technology. Applying this principle to firm governance, the firm restructured The Committee—now renamed the Executive Committee—to comprise three principals, representing the areas of project management, design, and production. (They would later be replaced with the "three best individuals" as identified by the directors.) These changes greatly enhanced collaboration within the firm and fundamentally changed the way SBRA designed and built buildings.

At the same time, SBRA revisited its approach to business development. With more firms competing for fewer projects, the firm's reputation and its longstanding professional and personal networks could no longer guarantee new business. It was now necessary to go out and sell the firm's services—to the initiated and the uninitiated alike.

Some of the principals actively engaged in marketing efforts. "I read some books and took a course in this new area people called 'marketing,'" Hugh Shepley recalled. "This gave me some ideas that I put into effect, like presenting the firm in the best light. I also took a couple of public speaking courses, which came in handy when dealing with potential clients."

Richard M. Potter, who had left in the late 1960s to work elsewhere, returned to SBRA in 1976 with interviewing techniques he had learned during his time away. "I saw that it's important to prepare for an interview by learning a lot about the interviewees and what they want," he explained. "It made a big difference, and we started winning jobs."

The firm also hired its first marketing consultant, Maximilian Ferro, a young staff architect. "Max did our first direct mail, targeting lots of hospitals," Smith recalled. "He stirred interest in Danbury Hospital, and we got the job as a result." Another major target was the academic client, and for good reason. Although virtually no American institution escaped the recession unscathed, those in higher education were among the hardest hit. Capitalizing on its success at Vassar, SBRA emphasized its expertise in renovating and recycling buildings. Work at various New England colleges and universities soon followed.

In 1977–1978, SBRA promoted Mathey, Acton, Leo McEachern, Potter, and Smith to principal. SBRA's in-house accountant since 1967, McEachern was the first nonarchitectural employee to reach this level. "Leo's promotion was a big event," Mathey explained. "It signaled a change in the way the firm looked at its leadership, and in our perception of the skills necessary to move the firm forward."

Andover Savings Bank, Renovation and Addition (left)
Margaret Clapp Library Addition, Wellesley College (above)

In 1978, the economy took another nosedive, with inflation spiking to 9 percent. To lighten the firm's burden, principals Richardson, Morss, and Clapp offered to retire early, while offering their services at no charge. The principals elected George Mathey SBRA's first corporate president. For the first time in its history, the firm's leader was not a Richardson, a Shepley, or a Coolidge. The financial turbulence of the 1970s had brought both the end to the family dynasty—and the beginning of the modern firm.

Mathey assumed his new position with a clear course of action. The first step was to bring in new work—and to get every architect, regardless of rank, involved in the effort. He issued a firm-wide memo:

Obtaining more commissions of the appropriate type and scope is the only way we can overcome this reversal. If any of you hear or read about potential new work or have any suggestions about improving our operation, please notify me as soon as possible.[10]

To make ends meet, the Executive Committee decided to reduce directors' salaries by 20 percent and associates' salaries by 10 percent, with no reduction in work hours—a substantial cut, considering that inflation during this period was in the double digits.

In another move to disperse responsibility, Mathey created opportunities for the firm's up-and-coming architects by placing them in charge of their own projects. As Squaw Valley—for which Mathey himself was project architect—and Pen Bay had demonstrated, the associates were the place to look for high-quality, innovative work and the next generation of firm leadership. The policy had immediate results: the number of projects grew, and the size of the firm as well. While the country was still in the throes of recession, SBRA needed to find a larger office.

Rebound: The Massachusetts Miracle

The leadership changes undertaken during this period helped carry SBRA through the economic difficulties of the late 1970s and early 1980s, and positioned the firm to prosper with the return of a strong economy. Anticipating large-scale expansion, in 1982 SBRA moved its offices from the Ames Building (its headquarters since the 1890s, and where it had sprawled over many floors), to the Insurance Exchange Building at 40 Broad Street, also designed by the firm. The new office was significantly larger and occupied only one floor—a layout that greatly facilitated collaboration.

The move was perfectly timed, for in the months that followed, the American economy set sail on a six-year boom of unprecedented size. Between 1982 and 1988, the Dow soared from 700 to 2,500. It was a time of easy money and rapid development—known locally as the Massachusetts Miracle, as the rise in the number of high-tech, knowledge-intensive companies made Massachusetts one of the fastest-growing economies in the country. During these years, SBRA expanded its practice within its core markets and moved into new geographic and client areas in order to support the needs of an increasingly diverse society.

In the early 1980s, the firm's health care practice flourished, with commissions at several smaller hospitals as well as larger medical centers in the New England area. Frequently, the project involved reno-

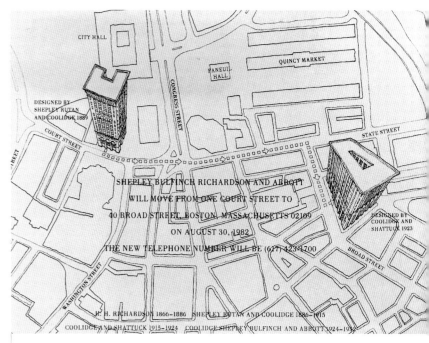

SBRA Office, 1982 (left)
SBRA Office Move, 1982 (above)

Sampson County Memorial Hospital (top)
Bertrand Library, Bucknell University (above)
Olin Library, Kenyon College (right)

vating or enlarging a 1960s-era building to better meet current needs. One of the firm's few projects outside New England, Sampson County Memorial Hospital in Clinton, North Carolina, resulted from the enthusiastic endorsement by the hospital administrator, who had worked with the firm at Pen Bay a decade earlier.

The sunnier economic climate also attracted renewed interest in SBRA's skills and experience from the academic sector. More often than not, the client was a small liberal arts college rather than a large university, and the project of choice was a library. Many of these new projects were directed by two young associates, Geoffrey T. Freeman, who by the late 1990s would have more than 70 libraries to his credit, and Paul Sun, who would make a name for himself as an outstanding designer.

While the firm continued to win library commissions close to home, it also began marketing its services outside New England. The Fackenthal Library of Franklin and Marshall College, in Lancaster, Pennsylvania (1983), represented the first major academic library project outside the region since 1912, when the firm built the William Rainey Harper Memorial Library at the University of Chicago. The F&M library led to a campus master plan there as well as a number of projects at Bucknell University in nearby Lewisburg. "It was unheard of in those days to go somewhere because of a client referral," Freeman recalled. "But the referrals came, and we went on to a number of other small and wonderfully visionary colleges outside New England, including Kenyon in Ohio and Hope in Michigan." (At Hope, the Van Wylen Library earned the American School and University Architectural Portfolio Citation in 1988 and the AIA/American Library Association Award of Excellence in 1989.) Many of these colleges became important repeat clients, providing SBRA with opportunities to design master plans, campus centers, science and engineering buildings, athletic complexes, and dormitories in the years to come.

Expanding Capabilities

To meet the needs of its expanded client list, SBRA enlarged and diversified its leadership. During the early 1980s, four architects were promoted to principal: Geoffrey Freeman, Mallory Lash, Gerrit Zwart, and Paul Sun, the first person of Asian descent to reach this position.

It was also during the early 1980s that African-American designer Ralph T. Jackson was promoted to associate and took the lead in some important projects, beginning with the Billings Student Center. (See below.) In the early 1990s, Jackson would become the firm's first black principal and would receive national recognition for his design capabilities, including an award from the National Organization of Minority Architects for his design of Cornell University's Carl A. Kroch Library. In 1999, he would be inducted as a Fellow of the AIA—a consummate honor accorded only a select number of architects nationwide.

To expand its design repertoire and its markets in the early 1980s, the firm for the first time looked beyond its walls for new leadership. Known for bold new approaches to health care facility design, Elizabeth S. (Zibby) Ericson became SBRA's first woman principal in 1983. In 1996, she was named a Fellow of the AIA, a notable accomplishment, considering that only 6 percent of all architects in the

Ralph T. Jackson, FAIA (top left)
Elizabeth S. Ericson, FAIA (top right)
Principals and Associates, 1982 (above)

United States at that time were Fellows, and that only 4 percent of that small number were women. Ericson's work at SBRA includes Children's Hospital, the New England Deaconess Hospital, and the Kent Hale Smith Engineering and Science Building at Case Western Reserve University. (See Chapter 5.)

The arrival in 1982 of H. Jan Heespelink broadened the firm's skills with corporate experience. Under his leadership, the firm undertook projects with Andover Companies, Fidelity, Simplex, General Electric, and Raytheon.

By 1984, the number of principals stood at 14. In this year, the firm also created the position of Senior Associate—another way of rewarding merit and, in some instances, selecting the next generation of leaders.

A Civic Statement in Washington

As SBRA expanded its regional reach in higher education and health care during the 1980s, it also found new design opportunities in the civic arena. The firm's most significant project of this kind is the Smithsonian South Quadrangle in Washington, D.C. An enormous complex consisting of the Arthur M. Sackler Gallery, National Museum of African Art, S. Dillon Ripley Center, and Enid A. Haupt Garden, the Smithsonian South Quadrangle is a study in how to do more with less—less land, that is.

The story begins with a man of enormous erudition and vision, Secretary of the Smithsonian Institute S. Dillon Ripley. During his more than 20-year tenure, Ripley was the principal force behind the construction, expansion, and renovation of several important museums, including the Hirshhorn Museum and Sculpture Garden, the Anacostia Neighborhood Museum, the Air and Space Museum, the Museum of American History, the Museum of Natural History, and even the National Zoo.[11] Having acquired the extensive Asian art collection of Arthur M. Sackler and the contents of the National Museum of African Art, Ripley needed a place to put them. The location on the Mall posed a challenge even for Ripley: how to design a building in the proximity of three landmark buildings, each with a distinctly different architectural style—the Castle, a Gothic Revival building designed by Renwick in the 1850s; the Arts and Industries Building, erected in the early 1880s; and the Freer Gallery of Asian Art, a late-Renaissance style building completed in 1921.[12]

The solution was apparent: underground buildings that would conserve open space and recreate a garden cherished by the community. Hiring Junzo Yoshimura, the architect to the emperor of Japan, Ripley instructed him to "divert the sound, the ambient noises of Independence Avenue, cut off the view of the Forrestal Building and the rest of the urban landscape across the street and preserve the peaceful mini-park atmosphere."[13] Yoshimura proposed small ethnically inspired pavilions, one a Japanese shrine, the other an African-style structure, each with a sunken courtyard.

Meanwhile, Ripley conducted a search for the firm that would work with Yoshimura. SBRA threw its hat into the ring and project manager Dick Potter put together a team of 13 different representatives capable of explaining every facet of the project to the government. "We went down to Washington two days before the interview and had four rehearsals," he recalled.

South Quadrangle, Smithsonian Institute (left top)
Cross-Section perspective of the South Quadrangle (left bottom)
Illusionist mural by Richard Haas, Central Concourse (above)

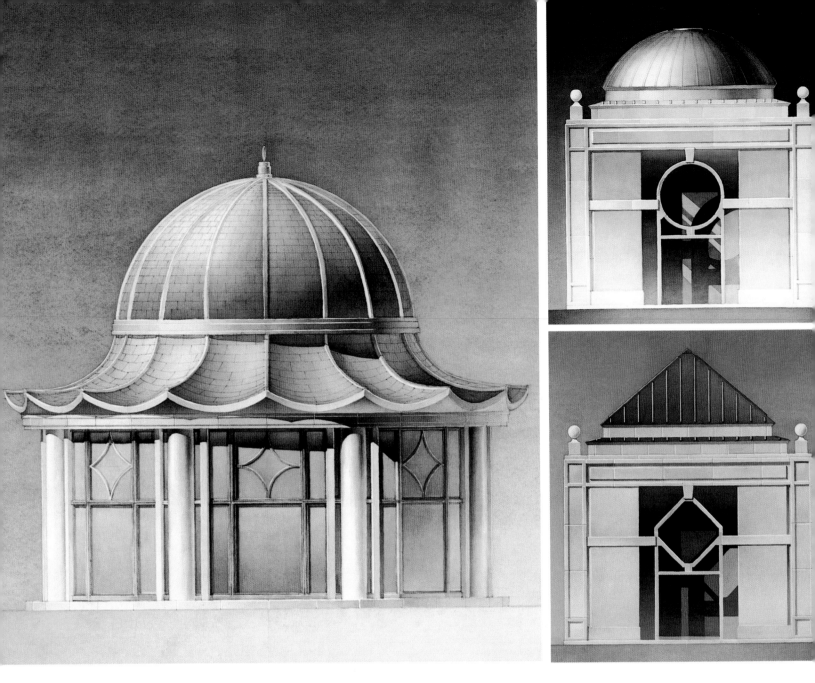

We were third of four teams to be interviewed. After it was over, we were told that they might let us know that day, but they might not. We were turned loose on the town and met later on the plane to return to Boston. We were all seated and ready to take off when the flight attendant called me to the front of the plane. She told me to call the Smithsonian. I was told that we couldn't go back to Boston because we had won, so I got off the plane.

Things, however, did not go as planned. Early in the design process, Yoshimura suffered an incapacitating stroke. "We were left alone to deal with seven commissions," Carlhian recalled. Completed after a lengthy review process by the General Service Administration, Carlhian's design differed significantly from the Yoshimura original. The two Beaux Arts-inspired pavilions—the beige granite Sackler with its hip roof and diamond-shaped windows, and the red granite African Museum with its copper domed roof and circular windows—took their cues from the adjacent buildings. (The revised design eliminated the sunken courtyards.) "The arcaded façade of the Freer dictated the fenestration of the African pavilion, surmounted by domes, while the fenestration of the Sackler took its cue from the roofs of the Arts and Industries Building," Carlhian pointed out. The preference for classical over contemporary was quite deliberate. "We did not know whether at some future date the buildings would be used for something else," he said. "We also did not want the buildings to look like creatures of the 1980s."

The pavilions, however, were only the first hurdle: there was still an enormous underground facility to redesign. "The challenge was to guide the public to the enjoyment of great works of art through a descending rather than an ascending procession," Carlhian explained. "One habitually climbs *up* to good things—to Heaven, to the altar, to virtue—while one goes *down* to hell, darkness, and the bathroom. Here we had to alter that concept. Our job was to lure people down to a matchless treasure trove." Generous use of skylights minimizes claustrophobic reactions to the subterranean structure.

In addition, there was the formidable challenge of underground construction. Because of the proximity of the Castle, the vibration from driving sheet pile, the customary method, would be too risky. The architects elected to use a slurry wall (a below-grade retaining wall) instead.[14]

The two upper floors house the Asian and African arts collections side by side, while the floor below houses the administrative space, exhibition, and educational facilities of the Ripley Center. The Sackler consists of a series of small, intimate spaces for displaying Oriental antiquities—jades, bronzes, and furniture. It employs the diamond motif throughout: diamond-shaped windows, and staircases angled right and left, leading down to a diamond-shaped reflecting pool. Its African counterpart, by contrast, houses big, open spaces better suited for displaying large works of art, and its circular stairwell leads down to a circular pool.

As the museum pavilions provide links between the buildings of the quadrangle, the gardens provide links between the pavilions and the collections lying below. The garden in front of the African pavilion features an Asian diamond shape, whereas the garden in front of the Asian pavilion is an African circle within a square. Between the two pavilions lies a formal Victorian garden, a recreation of the original.[15]

The Smithsonian South Quadrangle received numerous accolades, including awards from the Boston Society of Architects and the General

Kiosk watercolor (left)
Pavilion watercolors (left top & bottom)
Windows of the African Pavillion (above)

Services Administration. Critics were similarly enthusiastic. The *Washington Post* hailed the "designs for the visible parts of the Smithsonian Quadrangle—those huge new underground museums disguised on the surface as a couple of sedate little pavilions in a park—[as] exquisite in all respects."[16] "The new quadrangle at the Smithsonian," wrote Thomas Hoving, "…is a triumph of museum architecture and design. …Our best buildings are those that have the judgment, manners, and courage to harmonize and blend with their betters, those surrounding buildings created in a more sincere and thoughtful age. The Smithsonian's quadrangle is the latest addition to the short list."[17]

While every major commission brought SBRA increased recognition and visibility, the Smithsonian success brought a new national prominence for civic and cultural work. Other important public commissions soon followed, among them the Warren B. Rudman Courthouse in Concord, New Hampshire (1995). (See Chapter 5.)

Education in the Corporate Sector

Meanwhile, SBRA took advantage of the booming economy to return to the corporate market, which had not been an important area for the firm since the 1920s. The Management Development Institute for the General Electric Company provided the perfect opportunity for the firm to apply its extensive experience in academic design to a burgeoning trend in the business world, corporate education.

By 1982, GE was sending 5,000 of its new recruits and high-potential middle managers annually to courses at its Management Development Institute in Croton-on-Hudson, New York, the world's first major corporate business school. GE's new chairman, John F. (Jack) Welch, Jr., placed the institute at the center of a plan to remake GE by instilling corporate values of candor and aggressiveness in its employees.[18] To create a first-class educational environment for GE employees, Welch believed, "Crotonville," as the training center is known, needed additional housing.

GE turned to SBRA "because of its experience in designing college and university buildings and in developing campus plans that take advantage of natural site features," according to Bellamy H. Schmidt, manager of Crotonville's physical plant.[19] James Baughman, the director of Crotonville, knew SBRA's expertise in this area firsthand: before going to GE, he had been a professor at Harvard Business School, where he had worked with Jean Paul Carlhian on Baker Hall, an executive development residential complex. "GE was a wonderful opportunity," principal H. Jan Heespelink recalled. "It was an education project in a corporate setting, and a significant one at that. GE was a pioneer in having its own internal management school, and Crotonville was an important facility in terms of the company's culture."

With SBRA's assistance, GE built an entirely new residential building that contained 145 single bedrooms with private baths, a lobby, dining room, conference rooms, and recreational and support facilities. The plan also called for construction of a helipad and extensive landscaping. Design principal Jean Paul Carlhian broke up the new residence facility into six distinct units, each defined by a pitched slate roof, that followed the existing sloping topography of the 50-acre site and reinforced the feel of an established rural campus.

After completing the residence building in 1988, SBRA and GE

Residential Complex, General Electric Company (left)
Dining and Conference Facility, General Electric Company (above)

continued working together at Crotonville. "SBRA touched every building on the campus over the next 11 years," Heespelink said. "The firm's long association with GE gave SBRA credibility in the corporate sector."

As SBRA branched into new areas, a project in Vermont provided the opportunity to return to the firm's roots.

A Celebration of Past and Present

The Billings Memorial Library at the University of Vermont, H. H. Richardson proudly said, was "the best and most dignified design I have made for a building of its kind"—no small praise coming from the architect who had designed several outstanding libraries in the course of his career.[20] One hundred years after its completion, his firm returned to the site. In April 1986, the university dedicated SBRA's Billings–Ira Allen Campus Center, a structure linking Richardson's library (converted in 1963 to a student center) and its campus neighbor, the 1927 Ira Allen Chapel by McKim, Mead & White.

The new campus center, wrote George Mathey, was an inherently "fascinating project" for Richardson's successors. How often did they get the chance to integrate buildings by giants of American architecture—Richardson, the firm's founder, and McKim, Mead & White, whose principals had started out as his apprentices?[21]

SBRA's experience in adding to great works of architecture, most recently at Vassar College's Student Center and the Smithsonian, played an important role in the development of the design. Designer Ralph Jackson, who worked with Jean Paul Carlhian on the project, explained the underlying concept. "This was the first time I thought it would be brilliant *not* to do a building," he said, adding that the highly contextual project was an exercise in respecting tradition and hierarchy. "The addition needed to be sympathetic, but subordinate, to the existing buildings, the Romanesque library and the Georgian chapel," he said. The design therefore kept the roofline of the new campus center below the major architectural details of the older buildings and preserved the "view corridors," or space, between and around them, so that there was no compromise or alteration of their appearance from the campus green.

Jackson harmonized the disparate styles of the original buildings by incorporating motifs from each in the new addition. Thus, the roof and window forms of the dining pavilion echoed Billings's roof and fenestration, while the Colonial Revival style of the lecture hall came from the chapel. The bricks of the addition mirrored both the chapel brick and Billings's reddish-brown stone. "The result was a collage of forms and styles in response to context," Jackson said.

"The genius of the design," enthused Lattie F. Coor, president of the University, "is in its ability to unite an overused building with an underused one, spread the traffic evenly between them, and not mar the architectural or historic integrity of either."[22]

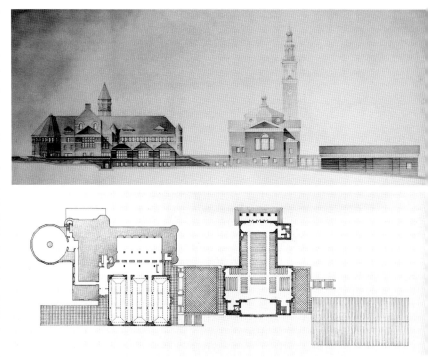

Billings-Ira Allen Campus Center (left)
Elevation of Campus Center (top)
Floor Plan of Campus Center (above)

Richard A. and Susan F. Smith Research
Laboratories, Dana–Farber Cancer Institute

Clinical Building, Deaconess Hospital

Library Building,
Albuquerque Academy

The Information Age

William A. Walsh Library,
Fordham University

Science Library,
University of California at Riverside

Irving S. Gilmore Music Library,
Yale University

5 | The Firm in the Information Age, 1989–1999

The last years of the twentieth century witnessed momentous changes in the world economy. The fall of the Berlin Wall and the end of the Cold War marked a new age in global politics, while the continuing revolution in information technology—television, computers, software, and telecommunications—helped transform virtually every aspect of modern life. The basis of the American economy shifted from manufacturing and an emphasis on maximizing production to services and meeting the needs of individual customers. Information became the key commodity, and flexibility and agility prevailed as the essential ingredients for business success as the marketplace grew in size and diversity. Both at home and abroad, corporations redrew their boundaries, joining forces with suppliers, customers, and even competitors to achieve economies of scale and to provide clients with a broader yet cost-effective range of services.

This new climate—the "knowledge economy"—affected all sectors of American enterprise, including the architectural profession. Clients became better informed about the design and construction of buildings than in the past and had a clearer understanding of their specific needs. On the supply side, the boundaries between once distinct services became blurred, and competition to plan, design and construct buildings grew more intense. Real estate, financial management, and management consulting firms began offering facilities planning and design services, while project management firms cast themselves as client advocates for project efficiency and cost control.

Cincinnati Public Library

To satisfy new marketplace needs, SBRA formed associations with a variety of architectural firms nationwide, thus sustaining the geographical expansion begun in the early 1980s without establishing another office. At the same time, the firm rethought its delivery of services, reviving and strengthening old areas of expertise, such as scientific research, and promoting new ones, such as interior design and master planning. To facilitate this expansion, SBRA found new and more effective ways of collaborating on projects within the firm, with clients, and with myriad service providers.

As in other fields, information technology played a central role in these developments. By 1982, when *Time* named the computer the "Machine of the Year" and the personal computer was rapidly becoming a fixture in homes and offices across the country, Computer Aided Design (CAD) was gaining currency in architectural circles. What first appeared at SBRA as a specialty run by one or two technical experts in a room apart from all the traditional design activity soon became a staple of every drafting station. "CAD helps the designer the way the word processor helps the writer in the creative process," explained design principal Ray K. Warburton. "The designer uses CAD to manipulate and refine his ideas to develop a design concept. He can take it from the most simple diagram and massing model to the most complex plan and rendering." CAD also considerably enhanced the collaborative process within the office and with clients. "CAD allows you to visualize a building and manipulate that image in real time with clients and reviewing authorities," explained principal Ronald Finiw. "It is a great tool for helping clients see and choose among different options."

With every technological advance, CAD played an increasingly important role, enabling SBRA to undertake larger and more complex projects with greater ease. The first project to employ CAD in virtually every phase of the design process was also the biggest in the firm's history: the Dartmouth-Hitchcock Medical Center (DHMC) in Lebanon, New Hampshire. This project spurred SBRA employment to beyond 200 and fortified the firm against the recession of the early 1990s.

Putting the Patient First |

"Rural New Hampshire and the space age meet head-on in the new Dartmouth-Hitchcock Medical Center—a high-tech medical complex, Pentagon-like in scale, gleaming white and colossal in the serenity of an evergreen forest," hailed the *New Hampshire Sunday News*.[1] Completed in 1991, Dartmouth-Hitchcock Medical Center houses the facilities of three independent institutions—the Mary Hitchcock Memorial Hospital, the Hitchcock Clinic, and Dartmouth Medical School—and serves the full spectrum of community and regional health needs.

This ambitious undertaking came at a time when the delivery of health care was changing dramatically. As the debate over managed care gained momentum in the 1980s, increasing numbers of hospitals pooled resources and placed greater emphasis on ambulatory care and preventive medicine in an effort to cut health care costs. These developments in turn caused a major shift in the focus of hospital design.

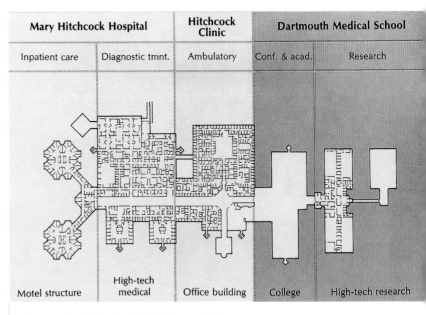

Dartmouth–Hitchcock Medical Center (left)
Comprehensive Floor Plan (above)

To survive in an increasingly competitive market, hospitals needed to be user-friendly facilities that attracted the consumer—patients and their families—who now could choose their place of treatment.[2]

SBRA was quick to see the potential that Dartmouth-Hitchcock offered. It was an opportunity to design a health care facility from the ground up, last done at Penobscot Bay Medical Center in the early 1970s. "Dartmouth-Hitchcock was the first project that really integrated a modern ambulatory facility, an inpatient hospital and a medical school," noted Mason Smith, one of two principals in charge of the project. "The SBRA team effectively engaged and challenged us," explained James Varnum, president of Mary Hitchcock Memorial Hospital. "They encouraged us to think about the tremendous opportunity we had before us. We knew they would help us take advantage of it."

"We realized that traditional inpatient facilities were dinosaurs," Smith explained. "It was clear that a strong focus on ambulatory care was integral to the modern hospital." This sense of purpose marked the project from its inception. "During the conceptual phase, we considered various alternatives," Smith recalled, "a plan good for physicians, a plan good for researchers, and a plan good for patients and their families. Everyone agreed that the patient came first. It was a new way of looking at hospitals."

The focus on patients and their families dominated most of the major design decisions, beginning with the mall plan itself: a "main street" linking five medical center buildings, interspersed with book and gift shops, a pharmacy, a food mart, an optical shop, conference facilities, restaurants, and a coffee shop. This clearly organized scheme facilitates navigation and thereby helps reduce the anxiety patients typically feel when going to the hospital. "Everyone is familiar with the idea of a mall," Smith said. "It signals that Dartmouth-Hitchcock is a welcoming place of health and community, not one of sickness and isolation." Noted design principal Lloyd P. Acton, "The building's architecture is a response to the hospital's philosophy."

"We knew that flexibility was essential, so we provided for an arterial system of horizontal and vertical circulation, to which one attached different modules that were open-ended," Smith said. "This allowed for the possibility of independent expansion without harming the original mall concept." Each of the five modules has different technical characteristics and capabilities: the Mary Hitchcock Hospital's inpatient and high tech medical units, the Hitchcock Clinic's ambulatory care building, and the Dartmouth Medical School's educational facilities and research laboratories. Frederick W. Nothnagel, Mary Hitchcock Hospital's vice president for facilities development, affirmed that the flexibility of the facility would make it easier for the hospital to stay on the cutting edge of technology.[3]

This modular configuration provided the basis for a novel organizing concept. Anticipating the need to link inpatient and outpatient facilities, Dartmouth-Hitchcock together with Hamilton/KSA, a health care consulting firm, developed a basic unit of program planning that replaced traditional medical departments with "clinical campaigns." Employing this concept, SBRA organized the campaigns horizontally in the inpatient, diagnostic and treatment, and ambulatory care buildings. Thus the "Heart" campaign comprises the inpatient unit; coronary and cardiovascular intensive care units; invasive and

The Mall at Dartmouth–Hitchcock (left)
Nurses' Station at Dartmouth–Hitchcock (above)

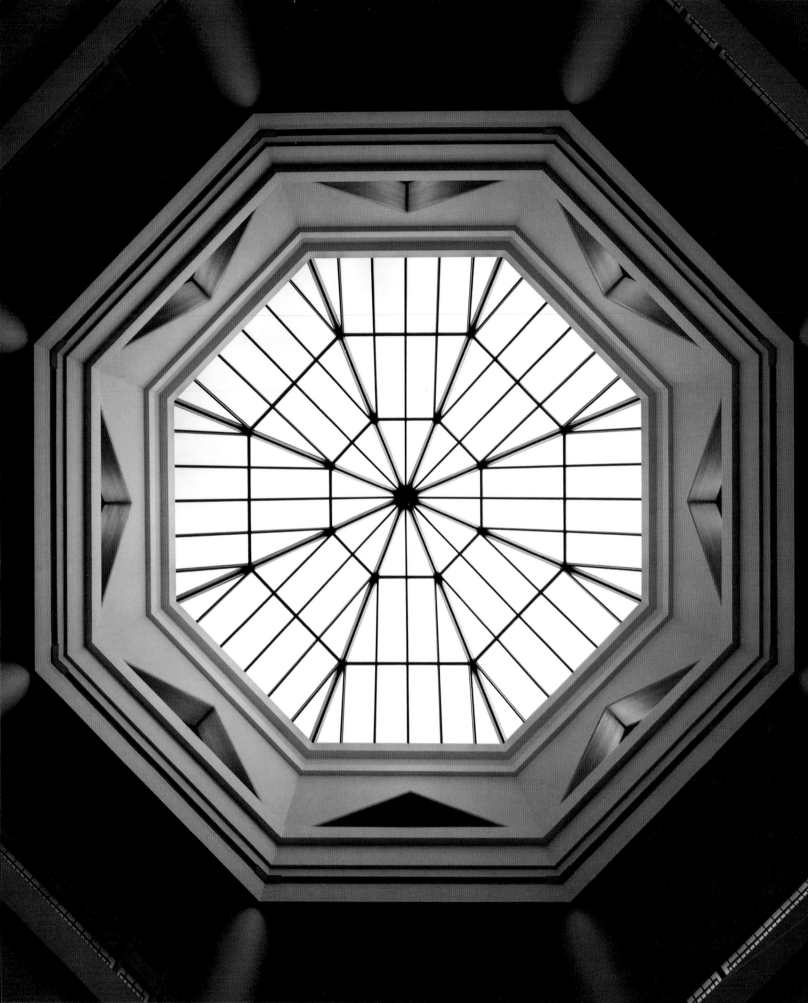

non-invasive suites for cardiology; and the cardiology, cardiothoracic surgery, and vascular clinics. All these are located adjacent to one another on one level. More efficient and economical for the medical center and less stressful for the patient, this arrangement emphasizes important horizontal connections and greater interaction among physicians and staff.

The increasing importance of ambulatory care also meant that the future inpatient population would require more intensive services. To meet this need, SBRA worked with Hamilton/KSA in developing the "pod" concept for the nursing units, where 36 beds are arranged in clusters of nine around each nurses' station. No bed is more than 15 feet from a station. This arrangement enables nurses to keep a closer eye on patients than in the traditional general medical/surgical nursing units, where large numbers of beds feed off a long hallway.

On the outside, Dartmouth-Hitchcock is at home in its wooded environs and on the inside, it is a place for people. "The mall gives you a warm feeling the minute you walk in," Varnum enthused. "It is a very friendly, comfortable environment. People are overwhelmed by the way we've put shops and restaurants right next to medical services. You wouldn't think you're in a health care facility at all."

Designing the Information Gateway

During this period, SBRA also responded to the academic institutions eager to incorporate emerging technologies into the delivery of education. A landmark case is the Thomas and Dorothy Leavey Library at the University of Southern California (1994). Just as experts were forecasting the potential of the Internet to bring limitless amounts of information into every residence and office in the years to come, the Leavey Library would demonstrate conclusively that the physical library—the real thing—would not, as a result, disappear. On the contrary, with the introduction of computing and electronic information services, the library would be revitalized as the intellectual heart of the academic community.

Leavey was to be a new kind of library, a library conceived as a "gateway to information," independent of format and location. "This was the first time a university asked SBRA to participate in the development of a programmatic idea," noted Geoffrey T. Freeman, the principal in charge of the project. "It was the first time we really asked ourselves the question, 'What is a library?' "

Finding the answer to that question was a process of intellectual discovery, analogous to what transpires in a library itself. "Before we began designing the building, we spent an entire year with various constituencies both within and outside the university, discussing what was happening to information technology, how it was coming into the library, and how people were using it," Freeman said. The SBRA team worked closely with Peter Lyman, a social scientist with expertise in the human dimensions of technology and a senior library administrator.

Lyman observed that learning is accelerated and intellectual curiosity is stimulated when students work together in groups around computers. This observation found expression at the heart of the new library, the "Information Commons," a technology center that provides access to print and electronic collections on campus and worldwide. With nearly one hundred group computer workstations and 21

Skylight at Dartmouth–Hitchcock (left)
Information Commons, Leavey Library (above)

workrooms ranging in capacity from 6 to 50, interaction and collaboration occur naturally.⁴ "Students wait in line to get into the Commons on a 24-hour basis," Freeman said. "It is a highly energized environment that is a very active component in the learning process." Convinced that demand for computing capabilities would continue to escalate, SBRA designed other areas of the library to accommodate technology-driven functions. Because group activity is by nature a barrier to individual study, students who want to work alone or in quiet use individual studies on Leavey's upper floors.

The building's success was immediately apparent—both to the USC community (with one million user visits in its first year) and to the outside world. In 1999, the Information Commons was expanded to twice its original capacity. "Leavey Library," one library expert wrote, is "the model for the transition from paper-based to digital research and scholarship. ...[Its] success as an information gateway has exceeded all expectations."⁵

"SBRA's own sense of its history made them want to understand our history and the context of our project," Lyman said. "The university needs to feel a sense of authorship," Freeman noted. "In the process of designing a building, we become part of the institution rather than a separate entity. Our role is to extend the institution, not make our little mark in history and then leave. We treat every building project in the same way."

From USC the firm went on to explore the development of new learning strategies and the impact of information technologies at several other colleges and universities. SBRA designed a new library at Fordham, and reconceptualized and expanded libraries at Emory, Dartmouth, and Rice. Freeman's work in library planning and design since the late 1970's positioned SBRA as a national leader in this arena. "Each project," he observed, "has provided us with learning that we can then bring to the next opportunity, reexamining and adapting it to suit the particular context. It's a very stimulating and rewarding process."

Preparing for the Future

Dartmouth-Hitchcock and other large projects helped sustain SBRA through the recession of the early 1990s. As a result, the firm was well positioned to exploit the boom that followed—a period of strong growth and low inflation the American economy had not seen since the 1950s. Strengthening its position further, the firm initiated a series of changes in management and organization to improve decision-making, promote collaboration both internally and with clients, and utilize its substantial knowledge capital.

The first step was to broaden the design leadership. In 1992 SBRA promoted designers Ray Warburton and Alexander Howe to Principal. With firm president George Mathey charting the course, the following year the directors formulated SBRA's first formal mission statement and a strategic plan outlining goals for the future. In 1994, the directors elected Mason Smith president to succeed Mathey. During the next five years, Smith led the directors in formulating and implementing initiatives to disperse management responsibilities more evenly, provide continuity of leadership, and adapt to changes in the marketplace. The directors (who are also principals in the firm) set

Thomas and Dorothy Leavey Library, University of Southern California (left)
Principals' Retreat, 1992 (above)

goals and priorities, while the Executive Committee, consisting of five directors elected by the entire board and representing a wide range of expertise, are responsible for the management of the firm on a day-to-day basis. Six councils, consisting of principals and associates, address firm-wide issues in the areas of design, production, project management, human resources, marketing, and information systems. In addition, the firm is now organized into client-focused practice groups: three primary groups (education, health care, and science and research), and two secondary groups (corporate and civic).

The firm is also exploring new ways of building business. A restructured marketing department is implementing an aggressive strategy to expand in SBRA's core markets and establish the firm's name in new ones. The firm's professional development program assures that principals, associates, and staff are well versed in the latest design technology and fully attuned to a fluid marketplace.

Pursuing New Opportunities

Ongoing changes in the delivery of health care led SBRA to expand its capabilities in hospital design during the 1990s. As the managed care revolution came to a head in the early days of the Clinton administration, hospitals nationwide either initiated massive cutbacks to survive or closed down entirely. Construction of adult inpatient facilities—consistently an important source of work for the firm—came to a virtual standstill. One type of medical facility, however, thrived during this period: pediatric hospitals, which because of shifting demographics—baby boomers raising families—enjoyed a demand not seen since the Baby Boom itself.

The design and operation of pediatric facilities had changed tremendously since the 1960s. With the realization that children had special needs and that the hospital environment needed to make them feel safe and supported, in the late 1980s and early 1990s pediatric facilities became more family-oriented and parents came to play a critical role in the healing process.[6]

In the mid-1980s, SBRA undertook a project of major proportions at Children's Hospital in Boston. Completed in 1988, the Inpatient Building became one of the first family-centered pediatric hospitals in the country and established SBRA as a leader in pediatric health care design. A large renovation project followed soon afterward at Yale-New Haven Hospital, where SBRA designed a wing devoted to women and children.

From there it was a short hop to Rhode Island Hospital—figuratively and literally. Wanting to reassert RIH's commitment to pediatric medicine, hospital officials decided to replace its aging Potter Building with an entirely new facility. The choice of architect was an easy one: SBRA had been RIH's principal architect for over 50 years, beginning with the Potter Building itself. For SBRA, it was an opportunity to take the ideas pioneered at Children's Hospital one step further—to design a hospital that developed family-centered care.

The new structure—named the Hasbro Children's Hospital in honor of the Pawtucket, Rhode Island toy manufacturer, Hasbro, Inc., whose generosity and fundraising activities made the project possible—was the result of collaboration by an extraordinary number of people. SBRA architects, Hasbro CEO Alan G. Hassenfeld, adminis-

Hasbro Children's Hospital (left)
The "Moongate" Entrance (above)

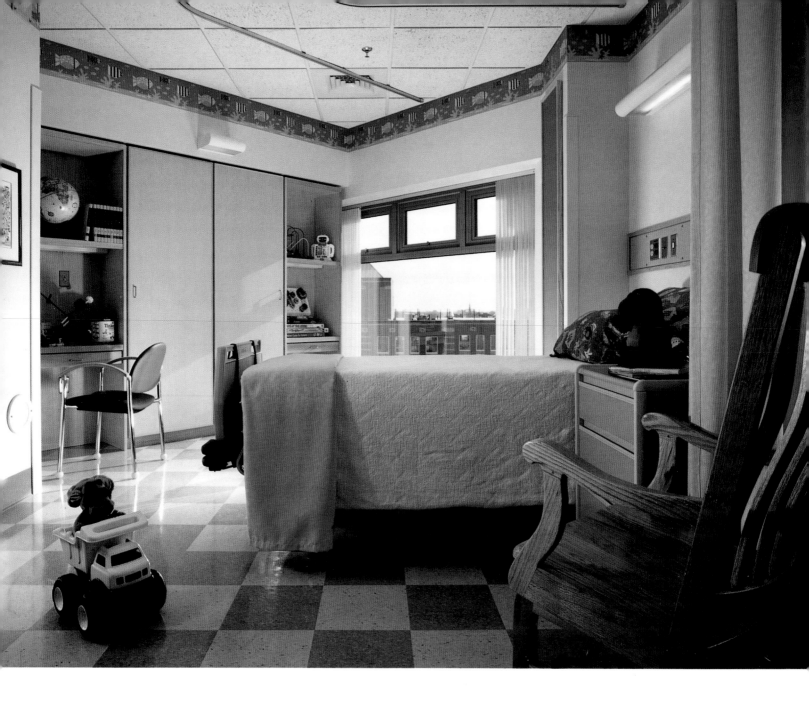

trators and staff from RIH, and parents and children from the local community all played a role in the design process.

Hasbro Children's Hospital is a state-of-the-art facility devoted to children and their families. The pink-and-blue-trimmed building stands like castle near the main artery into downtown Providence, creating a positive image for the child anxious about going to the hospital. On the inside, a child-friendly environment—featuring an interactive water sculpture and two-story gazebo in the lobby, patient floors designed as "neighborhoods," and a carpet patterned with footprints that aid in way-finding—says that this is a place for kids. Since parents play a critical role in their child's recovery, Hasbro has many features to accommodate parent needs, including daybeds and showers, kitchen facilities, and a "resource room," where they can read up on their child's illness and treatment options. "Hasbro was the first place where parents accompanied their kids into the operating room," noted principal William S. Mead. "The staff and doctors gave the family more control of their child's care, because this hastens the healing process."

A key figure in the project was SBRA principal Lloyd Acton, the designer of the Dartmouth-Hitchcock and Yale-New Haven facilities. A large, affable character—affectionately known around the SBRA office as "Uncle Bunny"—Acton was universally praised by hospital staff and parents for his flexibility and willingness to listen. When, for example, a parents group told Acton that the activity rooms were too small, he said, "Well, let's change it!" and redrew the plan, nearly doubling the size of the rooms and changing the shape of the building.[7]

In 1996, Hasbro received a citation award from *Modern Healthcare* and the AIA's Academy of Architecture for Health. "This hospital has features that appeal to all ages," noted one of the judges. "It delights the senses and creates a feeling of being cared for in a well-thought-out facility."[8] Three years later, Hasbro received an Honor Award for Design from the Boston Society of Architects and the Healthcare Assembly, which observed, "This building is remarkably successful as a facility for children, marked by playful elements on the inside and out. …This is an excellent project marked by smart planning, thoughtful interior design, nice detailing, and admirable design sensitivity to the user." But perhaps the greatest praise came from a young child who had been discharged from the hospital. "She burst into tears," Mead said, "because she didn't want to leave!"

Rejuvenating Old Structures

Whether to counteract the effects of time or accommodate the newest technologies, increasing numbers of buildings required extensive renovation or restoration. With the meteoric rise of the American economy in the 1990s, institutions that had long put such projects on hold now had the budgets to see them completed. SBRA was well equipped to respond to this growing demand. During this period, the firm renovated several buildings designed by notable architects of the late nineteenth and early twentieth centuries, including the Massachusetts State House on Boston's Beacon Hill, the Boston Public Library on Copley Square, and the Sterling Memorial Library at Yale University.

After more than 60 years of heavy use, Sterling Library—the heart of the prestigious university, the nation's second-largest university library, and the world's seventh-largest research library—was in criti-

Patient bedroom at Hasbro (left)
Lloyd Acton meeting with Hasbro's Staff (above)

Irving S. Gilmore Music Library, Yale University (above)
Sterling Memorial Library, Yale University (above right)
Carl A. Kroch Library, Cornell University (right)

cal condition. The central part of this Gothic structure, a "cathedral of learning" designed by James Gamble Rogers and completed in 1931, was a 16-floor book-stack tower, home to over 4.5 million volumes. Thanks to decaying pipes, broken windows, bugs and mice, and, worst of all, air—heat, humidity, and ultraviolet light—many books were turning to dust, or "yellow snow," as librarians called it.

The only option was a complete overhaul. With its experience in university library renovations, including Columbia's Butler Library (another Rogers design), SBRA was well suited for the project. The firm installed a climate-control system designed to minimize fluctuations in temperature and humidity, replaced 1,000 windows with insulating glass while maintaining their leaded-glass appearance, and provided a new roof and mechanical, plumbing, fire suppression, and electrical systems—all accomplished while the library remained fully operational. The renovations were completed in 1997.[9]

The following year, SBRA completed a related project, the Irving S. Gilmore Music Library, which transformed an overgrown light-well into a soaring multi-story reading room. Design partner Alexander Howe explained, "the Gothic-inspired steel trusses frame the space which is meant to recall the grand scale and ambiance of Sterling's other reading rooms." The facility provides a home for materials and functions previously located in four different places on campus. "The Music Library is more than simply a collection of books, scores, and recordings," noted University Librarian Scott Bennett. "It is a hub of musical activity on the Yale campus, an intellectual and creative commons for the many participants in the musical life of the University, a magnet for scholars from around the world to come to study music at Yale."[10]

During this period, the firm also designed major renovations and additions for several public libraries to accommodate the latest advances in information technology. The projects ranged from small-town libraries, like the Somerville Public Library outside of Boston, to large-scale urban projects like the Cincinnati Public Library.

Building interiors also felt the impact of technological developments. To respond to the increasingly complex task of interior design and provide a wider range of services to clients, SBRA strengthened its specialty in interiors. In the 1990s, its Interior Design Department contributed expertise on a number of firm-designed building projects, including Cornell University's Carl A. Kroch Library, Yale-New Haven Hospital, and Yale's Music Library.

Building for Discovery

The national prosperity that funded the renovation of old buildings also made it possible to build new ones. As universities across the country devoted more attention to scientific and medical research, SBRA secured several new opportunities in research facility design, a specialty dating back to the firm's work for the Rockefeller Institute and Harvard Medical School at the beginning of the century. A leading example is the Kent Hale Smith Engineering and Science Building (1994), Case Western Reserve University's showcase for its new multidisciplinary department of macromolecular science and flagship for the university's research efforts.

McKim Building Restoration, Boston Public Library

Senior administrators at Case Western (CWRU) approached SBRA with a clear sense of what they wanted in their new science building. "Frank Borchert, vice president for planning, had a vision about architecture," said design principal Elizabeth S. Ericson. "He believed the campus was in need of great buildings and spaces, and wanted to push the envelope and break conventional rules." CWRU's director of construction administration Karen Dethloff explained, "We wanted something forward-looking and cutting-edge that would reflect the work of the people who used the building, international leaders in their field."

The result was a building for and about scientific discovery. Capping the lobby of this unique structure is a large glass atrium whose glass sides slope outward and upward—a symbol of implosion. An enormous baldacchino, a modern version of a medieval altar canopy, breaks through the atrium roof and draws attention to the sky above, thus symbolizing the sacred entry into the domain of scientific research. "With its splayed walls and extended roof, this building symbolizes breaking out of the box, the continual questioning of conventional wisdom," Ericson observed. "Everything about this building invites you to explore."

Appropriately enough, a building in which different fields of science meet and work together emphasizes connectivity and community in a variety of ways. Clusters of offices, laboratories, and conference rooms wrapped around the atrium foster interaction among scientists, students, and visitors from the corporate world. Small staircases placed in the east and west wings encourage faculty to talk to one another. "We got rid of corridors, so there was no place to hide," Ericson said. "The day the building opened, one scientist looked down to the floor below and saw a colleague he hadn't seen in three years!"

"We didn't ask for everything—for example, the baldacchino—and at one point heavily scrutinized it for cost," Dethloff said. "In the end, we decided that it was important: it lets tremendous light into the building and is quite spectacular." She added, "SBRA followed the project all the way through to completion, and from start to finish had a sense of the big picture. This provided a level of continuity you don't see very often."

If public response is any indication, the building has succeeded greatly. "People have two very different reactions," Dethloff said. "Either they are completely perplexed or they love it"—the reactions a cutting-edge building is supposed to elicit. Described as a "bright, crisp, and pugnaciously unconventional structure" by one architectural critic, the building brings new vitality to an urban campus—a vitality apparent especially at night, when the atrium sparkles like a faceted gemstone.[11] "When the glass is all lit up, the building provides a sense of safety as well as a source of curiosity," Ericson said. "And that," she added, "is what science is all about."

In the years that followed, SBRA designed a number of other important research facilities, including the world-renowned Dana-Farber Cancer Institute Smith Laboratory Building in Boston. At the same time, the firm returned to another specialty of its past, civic architecture.

Rethinking the House of Justice

The New Hampshire Federal Judiciary wanted what all public servants want in a courthouse: a high-quality building that would return value within a publicly funded budget; a secure facility that would

Kent Hale Smith Engineering and Science Building, Case Western Reserve University (left) Detail of baldacchino (above)

protect the public and the employees of the court; and a design that would integrate new technology in an unobtrusive way. But the judges sought something else as well: a building that would symbolize justice.

"I served on the selection committee that chose SBRA," recalled United States District Court Judge Norman H. Stahl. "We were not sold a name: we got the distinct feeling that we'd get a lot of attention from them, and we had seen Jean Paul Carlhian's work at the Smithsonian and felt it was important." Enthused Clerk James R. Starr, "Every detail of our working life was discussed, considered, and incorporated in the final design."[12]

The judges came to SBRA with one specific request—that all the courtrooms have natural light. Eschewing the traditional arrangement that seated a judge's chambers directly adjacent to his or her own personal courtroom, the architects placed the courtrooms and chambers on different floors. This innovation made it possible to locate the courtrooms around the exterior of the building so that each receives natural light, making the courtroom livable and providing relief for trials that last all day.

In the most technologically advanced courtroom of the Warren B. Rudman U.S. Courthouse, two video monitors display the physical evidence to the jury, and in instances where there is a question of admissibility, they can relay that image directly to the Court of Appeals in Washington, DC. PCs, at every table for use by the attorneys and their clients, ensure that all parties, whatever their means, have access to the same resources. "The use of technology has saved the court approximately 20 percent of court time," Clerk Starr noted. "That's a significant savings for the taxpayer."

In response to recently implemented security requirements, the architects designed three banks of elevators to enforce absolute separation and provide a real sense of safety between prisoners, the judicial staff, and the public. Three separate circulation systems eliminate the possibility of a judge stepping into an elevator with the aggrieved family of a prisoner, and prevent the public from seeing detainees in shackles—images that might prejudice the jury.

The design conveys the courthouse's purpose through aesthetic means as well. Its tripartite massing symbolizes clarity and balance. Noted design principal Carlhian, "This building is about justice and rationality, right or wrong, innocence or guilt." Its interior sustains this theme, with a statue of Justice by sculptor Diana Moore and various related motifs—for example, an inverted semicircle cleaved down the middle to symbolize the sword of Solomon.

The Rudman Courthouse may serve as a model for courthouses in the twenty-first century. "We've been visited almost every week by people from other courts around the country," Judge Stahl noted. "People are struck by the fact that our courtrooms are wonderful and the benches work extraordinarily well. On more than one occasion, someone has pointed to one and said, 'If I could only pick this up and take it with me.' Now, that's a real compliment. But the proof of the building is when you live in it," he said, "and living in this building is easy."

Looking Ahead

In 1999, SBRA's diverse staff of nearly 200, led by 17 principals, is at work on a wide range of building projects—education, health care, scientific research, corporate, and civic—in every part of the country.

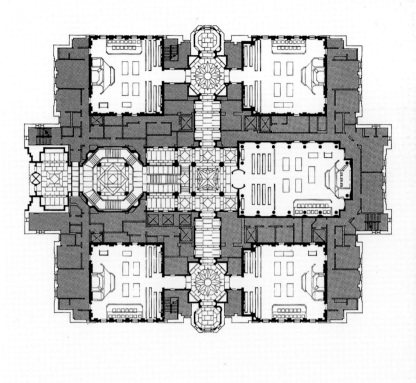

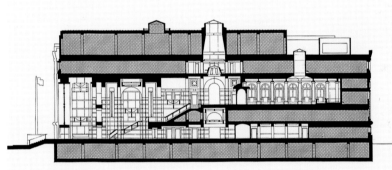

Main Concourse at the Rudman Courthouse (left)
Floor plan (top)
Section through Main Hall (above)

Rudman Courtroom Entrances

The extensive client list includes Bronson Methodist Hospital in Kalamazoo, Michigan, a master plan for Grinnell College in Iowa, the University of North Carolina's Science and Technology Building, Fidelity Investment Company's East Office Building in Boston, and the Eugene Public Library in Eugene, Oregon.

On the eve of the millennium, a longtime client provided an opportunity to build on work completed nearly 75 years earlier. In the 1920s, the firm helped Vanderbilt University realize its aspirations for a fully integrated medical school–teaching hospital complex. Since that time, Vanderbilt rose to the top tier of academic medical centers in the country, becoming renowned for excellence in pediatrics. In the late 1990s, Vanderbilt engaged SBRA to develop a conceptual design for a new freestanding pediatric hospital.

Vanderbilt and SBRA's other projects of the 1990s highlight significant themes in the firm's development during its first 125 years of practice. The firm has successfully adapted to meet the needs of a society that evolved from a regional industrial economy in the late nineteenth century to a global Information Age economy at the end of the twentieth. Making the transition in leadership, the firm has progressed from a practice run by a single great designer, to a family firm with a few partners, to a modern professional corporation. In a parallel development, the firm has enhanced its core design expertise with an array of services that includes master planning and interior design. The nature of the firm's relations with clients has changed also: what began as essentially a partnership between one architect and an individual patron like John D. Rockefeller, Charles W. Eliot, or George Canby Robinson has evolved into an collaborative effort involving numerous representatives from SBRA as well as the client institution.

SBRA's success is marked by important continuities as well. Today, as in 1874, the firm is known today for its insistence on the highest standards of architectural practice. As the awards and critical reviews over the years attest, SBRA consistently designs buildings appropriate for their time and context.

In addition, the firm's clients in the late twentieth century remain remarkably similar to its clients in the late nineteenth: they are important institutions, leaders in education, health care, scientific research, corporate and civic life. In some cases, the names have changed—from Frederick L. Ames to Fidelity, from Harvard to Rice, from the Rockefeller Institute to Case Western Reserve University, and from the Allegheny Courthouse to the Warren B. Rudman Courthouse. But SBRA continues to work with the best in their respective fields, and the best continue to seek the firm out. In the present, as in the past, Shepley Bulfinch Richardson and Abbott plays a vital role in giving physical expression to those institutions.

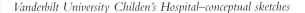

Vanderbilt University Childen's Hospital–conceptual sketches

SBRA 1999 · Nina Adams · Jennifer Aliber · Dana Anderson · Cheryl Andreas · Wagdy Anis · André Aoun · Hiroshi Asano · Garrold Baker · Sandra Barletta · William Barry · Jason Belanger · Paul Bell · Edward Benner · Christopher Bennett · Joseph Bettencourt · Jon Betts · Janette Blackburn · David Bliss · Nola Bonecutter · Amy Boring · Justin Boucher · Peter Bracciotti · Dawn Bridges · Michele Brooks · Renae Brown · Andrea Brue · Philip Burdick · Jeanne Carey · Jean Paul Carlhian · Daniel Ceglinski · John Christiansen · Bruce Cole · Peter Coletta · Kathleen Cotter · Wendy Daly · Christopher DeTore · Mary Ellen Devers · Tara Dirrane · Richard Donahoe · William Dovhan · Oliver Egleston · Kenneth Ellis · William Enestvedt · Elizabeth Ericson · Steve Erwin · Alan Estabrook · Karen Estabrook · Paul Fallon · Ronald Finiw · Daniel Fitzgerald · Laurel Franke · Geoffrey Freeman · Tom Frohlichstein · Nigel Gallaher · Anne Garrity · Walter Geribo · Andrea Giangrande · Claire Gilbert · Barbara Giurlando · Gary Glines · Duncan Grant · Richard Grinnell · Jonathan Gyory · John Hale · Itai Halevi · Charles Hayes · Jan Heespelink · Greg Heiges · David Hembre · Susan Hoadley · Brad Hörst · Alexander Howe · James Hunnewell · Sonny Inoue · Diana Jackson · Ralph Jackson · Shelley Johnson · Carolyn Judge · Leonard Kambarami · Eileen Keaffer · Thomas Kearns · Richard Keleher · Malcolm Kent · Steven Kent · Gina Kish · Sheila Kleinrichert · Katarina Krek · John Kucera · John Kuipers

· Joanne Kuo · Arto Kurkjian · Yar Laakso · Shaun Landon · Dohee Lee · Mima Leivi · Wei Li · Angela Lucien · Valerie Maass · Barbara MacCallum · Betteanne Macdonald · Sue Malomo · Margaret Manning · Kim Markert · Corina Martinez · Ana Martins · Kara Marziali · William Massey · Jordan Max · Rebecca McCarthy · Paul McIntire · William Mead · David Meek · Carlos Melendez · Jeffrey Mello · Katherine Meyer · Renée Mierzejewski · Christian Moneyhun · Kelly Monnahan · Anthony Morra · Eleanor Nichols · Lorrel Nichols · Christian Nixon · Peter Nobile · Derek Noble · James Oglesby · Charles Osborne · David Paarz · Bodil Pedersen · Diana Pomeroy · Bradford Prescott · Kenneth Propp · Uma Ramanathan · Steve Rigione · Robert Roche · Ruth Rogers · Joseph Rondinelli · Jonathan Ross · Visda Saeyan · Dan Salive · Alberto Salvatore · Rus Savary · Caroline Schwirian · Sinia Serrán-Pagán · Meg Shin · Allan Sifferlen · Leslie Sims · Adam Smith · Jessica Smith · Mason Smith · Cynthia Solarz · Susan Spaulding · James Spiegel · Michael Stephenson · Linda Swain · Michael Swanson · Sue Ellen Swinnerton · Chun Fa Tan · Salpie Tokadjian · Russ Tremaine · Kevin Triplett · Timothy Twomey · Helen Walker · Adrian Walters · Hai Wang · Ray Warburton · Michael Ward · Katharine Watts · Carole Wedge · Robyn Whittier · Wendell Wickerham · Eva Wong · Elise Woodward · Son Wooten · Steven Wychorski · Tang-Xian Xu · Richard Yeager · Hae Jin Yeo · Yeho Yin · Judith Yu · Gerrit Zwart

Notes | All dates provided for building projects refer to the completion of construction, unless otherwise indicated.

1. Establishing a Firm: Richardson and his Successors, 1874–1914

1   James F. O'Gorman, *Living Architecture: A Biography of H. H. Richardson* (New York: Simon & Schuster, 1997), p. 100.

2   The precise date of the founding of the firm is unknown. SBRA dates it to Richardson's move to Brookline in 1874 because it marked the beginning of a new phase in the architect's career.

3   Charles A. Coolidge, "Henry Hobson Richardson," in *Later Years of the Saturday Club*, 1864–1960, ed. M. A. De Wolfe (Boston: Houghton Mifflin, 1927), pp. 193–200. See O'Gorman, *Living Architecture*, p. 17.

4   O'Gorman, *Living Architecture*, p. 181.

5   George F. Shepley, Memorandum to C. A. Coolidge, 19 December 1886.

6   O'Gorman, *Living Architecture*, p. 185.

7   Coolidge to G. F. Shepley, 3 May 1886.

8   Jean Paul Carlhian, "Coolidge, Charles Allerton," *Dictionary of American Biography*, Suppl. 2 (12/31/40) (New York: Scribner, 1944–), pp. 117–118.

9   Coolidge, "Random Jottings – Mr. Charles A. Coolidge," n.d.

10 David Starr Jordan, *The Days of a Man, Being Memories of a Naturalist, Teacher, and Minor Prophet of Democracy*, Vol. 1 (1855–1899), (Yonkers-on-Hudson, N.Y.: World Book Co., 1922), pp. 374–75.

11 Coolidge, "Random Jottings."

12 Ibid.

13 Ibid.

14 Ibid.

15 Paul V. Turner, *The Founders and the Architects: The Design of Stanford University* (Dept. of Art, Stanford Univ., 1976), p. 46.

16 Jefferson Elmore, "A New View of Some Stanford History: What Mind Visualized Stanford Architectural Beauty?" *Stanford Illustrated Review* (December 1921), p. 153.

17 Charles H. Rutan to John K. Banner, 3 June 1910.

18 Andrew D. White, *The Autobiography of Andrew D. White*, Vol. 2 (New York: The Century Co., 1905), p. 448.

19 Elmore, "A New View," p. 153; Paul V. Turner, quoted in Peter C. Allen, "Preserving Stanford's Inner City," *The Stanford Observer*. (Jan. 1977), p. 4.

20 Allen, "Stanford University: An Academic Inner City," *Historic Preservation* (April/June 1978), p. 35.

21 Peter L. Donhauser, "Shepley, Rutan, and Coolidge," *Macmillan Encyclopedia of Architects* (New York: Free Press, 1982), p. 51. These buildings did not employ the steel frame construction that would soon revolutionize commercial building.

22 O'Gorman, *Three American Architects: Richardson, Sullivan, and Wright, 1865-1915* (Chicago: University of Chicago Press, 1991), p. 54.

23 Henry-Russell Hitchcock, *The Pelican History of Art. Architecture: Nineteenth and Twentieth Centuries* (Harmondsworth, Middlesex: Penguin Books, 1958), pp. 324–35.

24 John M. Hodgdon to J. D. Forbes, 14 January 1954.

25 Donhauser, "Shepley, Rutan, and Coolidge," p. 51.

26 James N. Wood, "The Art Institute of Chicago." *Museum Studies*, Vol. 14 No. 1 (1988), p. 5.

27 Lois Weisberg, "Welcome to the Chicago Cultural Center," Floor Plan (Chicago Department of Public Affairs, n.d.).

28 Russell Sturgis, "Shepley Rutan and Coolidge," *Architectural Record*, Vol. 6 (July-September 1886), p. 4.

29 In 1911, the firm was renamed Coolidge & Hodgdon. On Coolidge's retirement in 1930, it became a separate entity, Charles Hodgdon and Son, and was dissolved in 1944.

30 "Mr. Rockefeller's Institute for Medical Research," *New York Times*, magazine section, 10 December 1905, pp. 4-5.

31 John T. Bethell, *Harvard Observed: An Illustrated History of the University in the Twentieth Century* (Cambridge, Mass.: Harvard University Press, 1998), pp. 36–37. Eliot's upgrade of the medical school was part of a large-scale effort to revitalize Boston medicine and restore it to the prominence it had not known since the mid-1850s, when Massachusetts General became the first hospital to use ether in the operating room. The program also included plans for an affiliated hospital, to be built with funds from the Peter Bent Brigham estate and to bear his name.

32 Ibid., pp. 34–35.

33 Coolidge, "Random Jottings."

34 Ibid.

35 Ibid.

Notes cont.

36   Morris J. Vogel, *The Invention of the Modern Hospital: Boston 1870-1930* (Chicago: University of Chicago Press, 1980), pp. 80–87. In this period, the firm also designed the Rotch Memorial Hospital for Infants, which is now part of Children's Hospital. On the Boston Lying-In, also a firm design, see Chapter 2.

2. From World War I to World War II, 1914–1945

1   Sarah E. Rutan to C. A. Coolidge, 6 August 1914.

2   Rosemary Stevens, *In Sickness and in Wealth: American Hospitals in the Twentieth Century* (New York: Basic Books, 1989), pp. 57-58.

3   Ibid., pp. 17–18.

4   Morris J. Vogel, *The Invention of the Modern Hospital*, pp. 105–119.

5   Quote provided by the Boston Society of Architects.

6   The Boston Lying-In is now part of the Brigham and Women's Hospital.

7   Nelson C. Metcalf, "The Larger Lying-In Hospital," *Boston Evening Transcript*, 14 March 1917, part 2, p. 4.

8   For a detailed account, see Timothy C. Jacobson, *Making Medical Doctors: Science and Medicine at Vanderbilt Since Flexner* (Tuscaloosa: University of Alabama Press, 1987).

9   George Canby Robinson, "A History of Vanderbilt Medical School: History and General Description," in *Methods and Problems in Medical Education*, 13th series (New York: Rockefeller Foundation, 1929), p. 8.

10   Memo: Henry Richardson Shepley, November 1952, p. 1.

11   Otis Robinson himself was to become an architect and spend his career at the firm. He became a partner in 1968.

12   Robinson, *Adventures in Medical Education: A Personal Narrative of the Great Advance of American Medicine* (Cambridge: Harvard University Press, 1957), p. 159.

13   Jacobson, Making Medical Doctors, p. 121.

14   Robinson, "A History of Vanderbilt Medical School," pp. 1, 8.

15   Douglass Shand-Tucci, "Charlesbank Harvard: Radical Innovation, Architectural Masterwork," *Harvard Magazine* (Nov./Dec. 1980), p. 36.

16   Bainbridge Bunting and Margaret Henderson Floyd, *Harvard: An Architectural History* (Cambridge, Mass.: Belknap Press, 1985), pp. 178–79.

17   Ibid., p. 206 (quoting Julian Coolidge).

18   Shand-Tucci, "Charlesbank Harvard," p. 36.

19   Ibid.; Bunting and Floyd, *Harvard*, p. 197.

20   J. D. Forbes, "Shepley, Bulfinch, Richardson & Abbott, Architects: An Introduction," *Journal of the Society of Architectural Historians*, Vol. 17, no. 3 (Fall 1958), p. 11.

21   Bunting and Floyd, Harvard, p. 189.

22   Ibid.

23   James Ford Clapp, Jr., "Herman Joseph Voss: Distinguished Architect and Remarkable Man," n.d.

24   Alan Van Poznak, "The Last Smile of Skyscraper Romanticism," *Cornell University Medical College Alumni Quarterly*, Vol. 45, numbers 3/4 (December 1982), p. 14.

25   Both quotes provided in Van Poznak, p. 14.

26   Reginald Isaacs, *Gropius: An Illustrated Biography of the Creator of the Bauhaus* (Boston: Little, Brown, 1991, abridged edition), pp. 227–28. Gropius settled in the nearby suburb of Lexington.

27   James Ford Clapp, Jr., "Summary of B. B. Chemical Building," n.d.

28   Richard Kindleberger, *Boston Globe*, 22 December 1996, sec. H, p. 4.

29   Forbes, "Total Annual Commissions, Average Number of Employees Each Year and Number of Partners Each Year," 29 October 1952.

3. Postwar Reawakening, 1946–1972

1   *Boston Globe*, international airport section, 12 June 1949, p. 1.

2   *Boston Business Journal*, November 1950, reprinted in the *Journal of the Engineering Societies of New England*, Vol. 18, No. 34, 11 December 1950.

3   John D. Thompson and Grace Goldin, *The Hospital: A Social and Architectural History* (New Haven: Yale University Press, 1975); Stevens, In Sickness and in Wealth, pp. 213–55.

4   Sherman Morss, "Designing for Hospital Growth," *Trustee*, Vol. 33 (July 1980), reprint.

5   Richard M. Freeland, *Academia's Golden Age*: Universities in Massachusetts, 1945–1970 (New York: Oxford University Press, 1992), pp. 86-93.

6   John M. Bullitt, "The Eighth House," (October 1957), pp. 16–23.

7   The dispute was not resolved until the late 1970s, the university acquired the air rights and built the Kennedy School. See Bunting and Floyd, *Harvard, an Architectural History*, p. 275.

8   Ibid., pp. 262–63.

9   Lewis Mumford, "The Sky Line: UNESCO HOUSE—Out, Damned Cliché!," part 1, *New Yorker*, 12 November 1960, p. 129.

10 Joseph P. Richardson, Memorandum to the Directors, 5 January 5 1978.

11 Alis D. Runge, "Giant Display Case Shows Off Machines," *Progressive Architecture* (August 1969), pp. 87–89.

12 "1970 Honor Award Squaw Valley Cable Car Terminal," *New England Architect*, Vol. 1, no. 3 (June 1970), pp. 12–15.

13 G. E. Kidder Smith, *The Architecture of the United States*, Vol. 3 (Garden City, NY: Anchor Press, 1981), p. 196.

14 Francis D. Lethbridge, et. al., "1970 Honor Awards, Report of the Jury," *AIA Journal* (June 1970), pp. 79, 83.

15 Peter W. Huber, *Liability: The Legal Revolution and Its Consequences* (New York, 1988), pp. 3–18.

4. Embarking on the Next Century of Practice: Shepley Bulfinch Richardson and Abbott, 1973–1988

1   AIA Honor Award, 1973.

2   Joseph P. Richardson and Sherman Morss, Memorandum to All SBRA Stockholders, 17 April 1974.

3   William Marlin, "Hospitals: How Are They?" *Architectural Record* (August 1977), pp. 122–24.

4   Jean Paul Carlhian to Ada Louise Huxtable, 8 March 1977, pp. 1–2.

5   Carleton Knight III, "Old & New: Design Relationships in Architecture," National Trust for Historic Preservation, *A Preservation News Supplement* (April 1978), p. 2.

6   Gary Decker, "Vassar Center: Welcome to an Archexemplary Model," *Poughkeepsie Observer*, 8 January 1976, p. 7.

7   AIA Honor Award, 1977.

8   See Mildred F. Schmertz, "New Life for Old Buildings: Three Additions by SBR&A," *Architectural Record* (July 1975), pp. 89–98.

9   Richardson, Memorandum to the Directors, 5 January 1978, p. 1.

10 George R. Mathey, Memorandum, 20 June 1978.

11 Mary Ann Tighe, "The Quadrangle Comes Full Circle," *Northwest Orient Magazine* (March 1984), p. 42.

12 Donald Canty, "Masterful Placemaking Beside the Mall," *Architecture* (November 1987), p. 42.

13 Tighe, "The Quadrangle," p. 48.

14 Rose Thomas, ' "Invisible" museum attracts national attention,' *Building & Construction* (March 1988), reprint, pp. 2–4.

15 Canty, "Masterful Placemaking," pp. 44–46. For a fuller account of this project, see Edwards Park and Jean Paul Carlhian, *A New View from the Castle* (Washington, D.C.: Smithsonian Institution Press, 1987).

16 Benjamin Forgey, "Smithsonian Notes from Underground," *Washington Post*, 10 July 1982, sec. C, p. 1.

17 Thomas Hoving, "My Eye: Beauty and the Basement," *Connoisseur* (December 1987), pp. 35–38.

18 L. Landro, "GE's Wizards Turning from the Bottom Line to Share of the Market," *Wall Street Journal*, 12 July 1982, pp. 1, 16; R. Mitchell and J. H. Dobrzynski, "Jack Welch Reinvents GE," *Best of Business Quarterly*, pp. 60–67 (*Business Week* reprint, 14 December 1987).

19 V. Grinager, "Multi-Million Dollar Expansion Proposed by General Electric," *Gannett Westchester Newspapers*, 18 November 1983, sec. A, p. 3.

20 H. H. Richardson to Matthew Buckham, 5 July 1883.

21 Mathey to Larry Snyder, 27 May 1981.

22 Lattie F. Coor, University of Vermont publicity pamphlet, n. d.

5. The Information Age, 1989–1999

1 Nancy Meersman, "High Tech Medical Center in Green Oasis," *New Hampshire Sunday News*, special medical center section, 13 October 1991, p. 2.

2 C. Robert Horsburgh, Jr., "Healing by Design," *New England Journal of Medicine* (14 September 1995), p. 735.

3 Meersman, "High-Tech Medical Complex," p. 11.

4 Geoffrey T. Freeman, "The Academic Library in the 21st Century: Partner in Education," paper presented at the ALA/LAMA President's Program—"Library Buildings for the 21st Century," New York City, July 7, 1996; Deborah Holmes-Wong, Marianne Afifi, Shahla Bahavar, and Xioyang Liu, "If You Build It, They Will Come: Spaces, Values, and Services in the Digital Era," *Library Administration & Management*, Vol. 11, No. 2 (Spring 1997), p. 76.

5 Holmes-Wong et. al., "If You Build It," pp. 11–12.

6 Laura Hunt, "Easing Childhood Ills: Pediatrics in the 21st Century," *East Greenwich, RI Monthly*, (December 1993), p. 1; Susan Diesenhouse, "Suffering of Children Is Eased as Hospitals Change to Keep Families Near," *New York Times*, 14 December 1988.

7 Douglas Hadden, "Children's Hospital Reflects Hasbro Whimsy," *Times* (Pawtucket, RI), business section, 20 January 1994, p. 7.

8 BSA /Healthcare Assembly Award, 1999; Claudia Pinto, "Going Natural by Design," *Modern Healthcare* (November 1996), p. 42.

9 Annie Murphy Paul, "Library Time," *Yale Alumni Magazine* (December 1995), p. 42; no author, "Renovations and Innovations at the Yale Library," *Yale Bulletin & Calendar*, Vol. 24, No. 13 (4–11 December 1995), p. 1.

10 Paul, "Library Time," p. 42; "Music Library," *Yale Alumni Magazine* (November 1997), p. 12; "Renovations and Innovations," p. 5.

11 Steven Litt, "CWRU's Bright and Sassy Addition," *Plain Dealer*, 1995, section K, p. 3.

12 James R. Starr to Kevin Triplett, 21 October 1998.

Selected Bibliography |

General

Hitchcock, Henry-Russell. *The Architecture of H. H. Richardson and his Times*. New York: Museum of Modern Art, 1936 (and reprint).

_____. *A Guide to Boston Architecture 1637–1954*. New York: Reinhold Publishing Corporation, 1954.

_____. *The Pelican History of Art: Architecture: Nineteenth and Twentieth Centuries*, 3rd edition. Harmondsworth, Middlesex: Penguin Books Ltd., 1971.

Shepley Bulfinch Richardson and Abbott

Shepley Bulfinch Richardson & Abbott, Incorporated 1972 (undated).

Forbes, J. D. "Shepley, Bulfinch, Richardson & Abbott, Architects: An Introduction," *Journal of the Society of Architectural Historians*, vol. XVII, no. 3 (Fall 1958).

H. H. Richardson

Gill, Brendan. "A Fast Full Life," *The New Yorker* (February 9, 1998), pp. 79–80.

Ochsner, Jeffrey Karl. *H. H. Richardson, the Complete Architectural Works*. Cambridge, Mass.: MIT Press, 1982.

O'Gorman, James F. *H. H. Richardson: Architectural Forms for an American Society*. Chicago and London: University of Chicago Press, 1987.

_____. *Three American Architects: Richardson, Sullivan, and Wright, 1865-1915*. Chicago and London: University of Chicago Press, 1991.

_____. *Living Architecture: A Biography of H. H. Richardson* (Simon & Schuster: New York, 1997).

Van Rensselaer, Mariana Griswold. *Henry Hobson Richardson and His Works*. Boston: Houghton Mifflin, 1888 (and reprints).

Wilson, Richard Guy. "He Looked Like His Buildings," *Preservation* (January/February 1998), pp. 86–87.

SBRA's clients

Bunting, Bainbridge and Floyd, Margaret Henderson. *Harvard: An Architectural History*. Cambridge, Mass.: Belknap Press, 1985.

Freeland, Richard M. *Academia's Golden Age: Universities in Massachusetts, 1945–1970*. New York: Oxford University Press, 1992.

Stevens, Rosemary. *In Sickness and in Wealth: American Hospitals in the Twentieth Century*. New York: Basic Books, 1989.

Vogel, Morris J. *The Invention of the Modern Hospital: Boston 1870–1930*. Chicago: University of Chicago Press, 1980.

Index cont.

Abbreviations:

(t) top, (b) bottom, (l) left, (r) right, (c) center

Photographers:

Richard Cheek, pages 10, 127; Burr A. Church, page 50; Charles A. Coolidge, page 42(l); Steve Dunwell, pages 9(r), 22, 24; Esto Photographics, Peter Aaron, pages 4, 111(r), 126(l,t), 126(r,c); Esto Photographics, Jeff Goldberg, pages 111(l), 112, 126(b); F.L. Fales, page 53(t); Sigurd Fischer, pages 38(r), 39(l), 53(b), 63, 68(t); Gottscho-Schleisner, pages 64(l), 64(r), 65(c), 69, 75(t), 76, 77, 78, 79; Clyde Hare, page 20; Arthur C. Haskell, pages 39(c), 49; Hedrich-Blessing, pages 8(r), 30; Timothy Hursley, pages 119, 128, 129; Phokion Karas, page 80; Margaret Lampert, page 136; Lautman Photography, page 86(c); Larry Lawfer, pages 101(l,t), 101(r,t); John Edward Linden, page 111(c); Richard Mandlekorn, pages 110(l), 110(c); Robert Miller, page124(l,b); Robert Reck, page 110(r); Steve Rosenthal, pages 90(t), 90(b), 92; Gordon Schenck, Jr, pages 100(l,t); Julius Schulman, pages 66, 82, 84; Jean M. Smith, pages 87(r), 100(l,c), 114, 116, 117, 118, 120, 122, 123; Ezra Stoller, pages 9(c), 64(c), 65(l), 65(r), 94; Tebbs & Knell, Inc, pages 46, 48; Paul J. Weber, pages 38(l), 39(r), 40, 55(b), 58(t), 60, 61; Nick Wheeler, pages 6, 74, 86(l), 86(r), 87(l), 87(c), 88, 96, 97, 100(r,b), 103, 106, 107, 108, 130, 132(l), 132(r), 133(l), 133(r); Harold A. Willoughby, page 58(b)

Artists:

D.A. Gregg, pages 27(t), 27(b); Wei Li, pages 134, 135; H.R. Shepley, page 16; Paul Sun, page 102(c,b); US Postal Service, William G. Smith, page 12; Herman Voss, pages 38(c), 45(t); Shu-xiang Xi, pages 104(r,t), 104(l,t), 104(r,b), 109(t)

Sources:

Department of Printing and Graphic Arts, Houghton Library, Harvard University, pages 14(t), 14(b); SBRA Archives, pages 8(l), 8(c), 9(l), 13, 15(r), 17(l), 17(r), 18, 19, 21(t), 21(b), 23, 25, 26, 28(t), 28(b), 29, 31, 32-33, 34, 35, 36, 37, 43, 44(t), 44(l,b), 44(r,b), 45(b), 47(t), 47(l,b), 47(r,b), 51(l), 51(r), 52, 54, 55(t), 56, 57, 59, 62, 68(b), 70, 71(l,t), 71(c,t), 71(r,t), 71(b), 72, 73, 75(b), 81(l,t), 81(r,t), 81(b), 83, 85, 91(t), 91(b), 93, 95, 98, 99, 101(b), 102(c,t), 105, 109(b), 115, 121, 125, 131(t), 131(b); ©1999 USPS. All rights reserved, page 12; *Worcester: Its Past and Present*, 1888, page15(l)

About the Author

Julia Heskel is a consultant at The Winthrop Group, Inc., a firm in Cambridge, Massachusetts, that specializes in business and technology history. She is the author of several articles on Greek and Roman history and *The North Aegean Wars, 371-360 B.C.* (Franz Steiner, 1997), and is the co-author (with Davis Dyer) of a forthcoming history of Phillips Exeter Academy.

Acknowledgments

Many people helped make this book possible. I start by thanking the present leadership of Shepley Bulfinch Richardson and Abbott: firm president W. Mason Smith III, and directors Wagdy A.Y. Anis, Garrold E. Baker, Paul E. Bell Jr., Oliver W. Egleston, Elizabeth S. Ericson, Ronald T. Finiw, Geoffrey T. Freeman, H. Jan Heespelink, Alexander Howe, James F. Hunnewell Jr., Ralph T. Jackson, William S. Mead, Carlos E. Melendez, Jonathan D. Ross, Timothy R. Twomey, and Ray K. Warburton. The current and former directors of the firm devoted substantial blocks of time to oral history interviews and provided enthusiastic support for the book as a whole.

The Book Committee—principals Jonathan D. Ross and Ralph T. Jackson, Director of Marketing Katharine L. Watts, SBRA Librarian Katherine Meyer, and SBRA Archivist Robert J. Roche—poured tremendous energy into the project. They facilitated interviews, assisted with research, reviewed drafts, synthesized comments from other readers, selected photographs, and offered encouragement. Working with the SBRA team was a true pleasure.

The book also benefited from the attention of four readers who generously offered their insights on the architectural profession, SBRA, and stylistic matters. At SBRA, Mason Smith and Geoffrey Freeman read several versions of the draft. Outside experts James F. O'Gorman, the Grace Slack McNeil Professor of the History of American Art at Wellesley College, read Chapters 1 and 2, and Karen Cord-Taylor, editor of the *Beacon Hill Times*, made comments of a more general nature.

Lance Wickens gave the manuscript a close copy-editing and offered many good suggestions.

At The Winthrop Group, Inc., Founding Director Davis Dyer lent his knowledge of business history and provided invaluable aid throughout the production process, from the first outline to the final draft. Emily Wheeler conducted research and interviews and drafted background material on several different building projects.

This book was designed by Pentagram Design, Inc. of New York.

Oral History Interviews

SBRA

Wagdy A.Y. Anis, Garrold E. Baker, Jean Paul Carlhian, Elizabeth S. Ericson, Ronald T. Finiw, Geoffrey T. Freeman, H. Jan Heespelink, Alexander Howe, Ralph T. Jackson, Leo McEachern, George R. Mathey, William S. Mead, Richard M. Potter, Otis Robinson, Jonathan D. Ross, Hugh Shepley, W. Mason Smith III, Timothy R. Twomey, Kevin Triplett, Ray K. Warburton, Gerrit W. Zwart

Clients

Karen L. Dethloff (Case Western Reserve University)
Lloyd Hughes (Rhode Island Hospital)
Peter Lyman (University of Southern California)
The Honorable Norman H. Stahl (Warren B. Rudman Courthouse)
James R. Starr (Warren B. Rudman Courthouse)
James Varnum (Dartmouth-Hitchcock Medical Center)

1952 Wellesley College, Bates and Freeman Halls, Wellesley, MA
1953 Logan International Airport, Apron Building, Boston, MA
1953 New England Deaconess Hospital, Farr Building, Boston, MA
1954 Arthur Fiedler Footbridge, Boston, MA
1955 Northeastern University, Cabot Physical Education Center, Boston, MA
1956 Northeastern University, Hayden Hall, Boston, MA
1958 Rhode Island Hospital, Main Building, Providence, RI
1959 Harvard University, Quincy House, Cambridge, MA
1959 Rhode Island Hospital, George Building, Providence, RI
1959 Wellesley College, Margaret Clapp Library Addition, Wellesley, MA
1961 Harvard University, Leverett House Towers, Cambridge, MA
1961 Wellesley College, McAfee Hall, Wellesley, MA
1965 Cincinnati General Hospital, Emergency Department, Cincinnati, OH
1967 Smith College, Science Center, Northampton, MA
1968 Squaw Valley, Tramway, Tahoe City, CA
1969 Brown University, Graduate Center Dormitory, Providence, RI
1969 Middlebury College, Johnson Music and Arts Building, Middlebury,VT
1970 Cincinnati General Hospital, Main Building, Cincinnati, OH
1971 Winterthur Museum, Library, Winterthur, DE
1972 New England Deaconess Hospital, Farr Building Additions, Boston, MA
1973 Charles F. Hurley Employment Security Building, Boston, MA
1974 Walkers Art Gallery Addition, Baltimore, MD
1975 Bunker Hill Community College, Charlestown, MA
1975 Dartmouth College, Sherman Fairchild Physical Sciences Center, Hanover, NH
1976 Penobscot Bay Medical Center, Rockport, ME
1976 Rhode Island Hospital, Ambulatory Patient Center, Providence, RI
1976 Vassar College, College Center, Poughkeepsie, NY
1977 Wellesley College, Margaret Clapp Library Addition, Wellesley, MA
1983 Bristol County Courthouse, New Bedford, MA
1983 Franklin and Marshall College, Fackenthal Library, Lancaster, PA
1984 Boston Public Library Restoration, Boston, MA
1985 Old South Church, Sanctuary Renovation, Boston, MA
1986 Kenyon College, Olin and Chalmers Libraries, Gambier, OH
1986 University of Vermont, Billings–Ira Allen Campus Center, Burlington,VT
1988 Children's Hospital, Ipatient Building, Boston, MA

1960

1970

1980